HARCOURT

Math

Challenge
Workbook

Grade 1

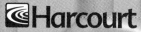

Orlando   Austin   Chicago   New York   Toronto   London   San Diego

Visit *The Learning Site!*
www.harcourtschool.com

Copyright © by Harcourt, Inc.

All rights reserved. No part of this publication may be reproduced or transmitted
in any form or by any means, electronic or mechanical, including photocopy,
recording, or any information storage and retrieval system, without permission
in writing from the publisher.

Permission is hereby granted to individual teachers using the corresponding student's
textbook or kit as the major vehicle for regular classroom instruction to photocopy
Copying Masters from this publication in classroom quantities for instructional use and
not for resale. Requests for information on other matters regarding duplication of this
work should be addressed to School Permissions and Copyrights, Harcourt, Inc.,
6277 Sea Harbor Drive, Orlando, Florida 32887-6777. Fax: 407-345-2418.

HARCOURT and the Harcourt Logo are trademarks of Harcourt, Inc., registered in
the United States of America and/or other jurisdictions.

Printed in the United States of America

ISBN 0-15-336503-X

1 2 3 4 5 6 7 8 9 10 054 10 09 08 07 06 05 04 03

CONTENTS

© Harcourt

© Harcourt

© Harcourt

© Harcourt

Model More Addition Stories

Draw pictures. Write how many there are in all.

1.

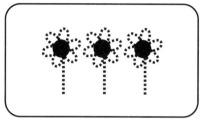 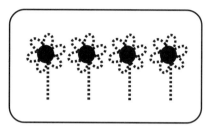

3 flowers   4 flowers   __7__ in all

2.

2 dogs   3 dogs   _____ in all

3.

3 birds   3 birds   _____ in all

4.

4 ducks   2 ducks   _____ in all

© Harcourt

Name _____

Use Symbols to Add

Write the numbers. Circle the sum.

1.

__1__ + __3__ = (__4__)

2.

____ + ____ = ____

3.

____ + ____ = ____

4.

____ + ____ = ____

5.

____ + ____ = ____

6.

____ + ____ = ____

© Harcourt

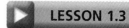

Add 0

Draw to show the numbers.
Add 0. Write the sum.

1.

$$3 + 0 = \underline{3}$$

2.

$$2 + 0 = \underline{}$$

3.

$$5 + 0 = \underline{}$$

4.

$$4 + 0 = \underline{}$$

5.

$$1 + 0 = \underline{}$$

6.

$$6 + 0 = \underline{}$$

© Harcourt

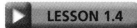

Missing Pieces

Draw pictures.
Then complete the number sentence.

1. 2 blue birds fly.
   2 red birds join them.
   How many birds in all?

   ___ + 2 = 4

2. David saw 1 white rabbit.
   Then he saw 3 brown rabbits.
   How many rabbits did he see
   in all?

   ___ ◯ 3 ◯ ___

3. 3 green ducks swim.
   1 white duck joins them.
   How many ducks in all?

   ___ ◯ ___ ◯ 4

4. How are all these number sentences the same?

   _____

   _____

   _____

© Harcourt

Name _____

Blast Off!

Write the sums. Circle each animal whose sums are the same. Draw those animals in your spaceship.

1.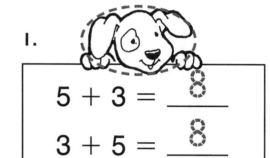

$5 + 3 =$ ___ 8

$3 + 5 =$ ___ 8

2.

$2 + 3 =$ ___

$3 + 2 =$ ___

3.

$3 + 4 =$ ___

$4 + 3 =$ ___

4.

$2 + 6 =$ ___

$6 + 2 =$ ___

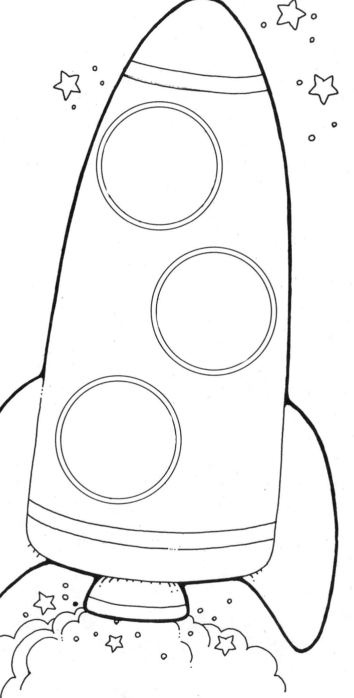

Addition Combinations

Draw things to show ways to make the sum.
Complete the addition sentence.

1.

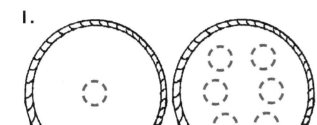

$\underline{1} + \underline{6} = \underline{7}$

2.

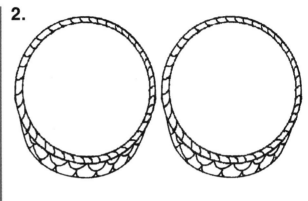

$\underline{} + \underline{} = \underline{7}$

3.

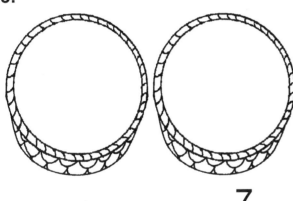

$\underline{} + \underline{} = \underline{7}$

4.

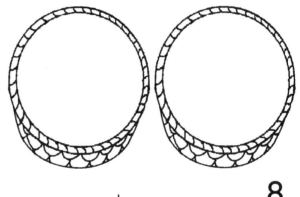

$\underline{} + \underline{} = \underline{8}$

5.

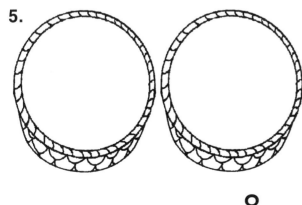

$\underline{} + \underline{} = \underline{8}$

6.

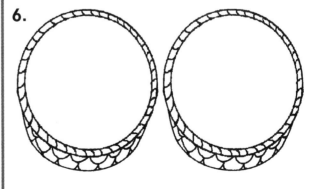

$\underline{} + \underline{} = \underline{8}$

CW6   Challenge

© Harcourt

More Addition Combinations

Circle the ways to make each sum.

7	8	9	10
(6 + 1)	2 + 4	9 + 0	9 + 1
5 + 3	4 + 4	2 + 7	7 + 3
2 + 5	6 + 1	3 + 5	2 + 6
3 + 3	7 + 1	8 + 1	6 + 4
2 + 4	4 + 3	4 + 5	2 + 8
7 + 0	3 + 5	1 + 7	5 + 3
0 + 5	6 + 2	2 + 4	3 + 7
7 + 2	0 + 8	4 + 1	5 + 5
4 + 3	2 + 5	6 + 3	0 + 9

© Harcourt

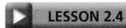

Vertical Addition

Circle the two problems that
you think have the same sum.
Then write the sums to find out.

1.

(3 + 4 = 7)   4 + 1 = 5

$$\begin{array}{r} 3 \\ +4 \\ \hline 7 \end{array}$$

2.

2 + 6 = ___   2 + 4 = ___

$$\begin{array}{r} 2 \\ +6 \\ \hline \end{array}$$

3

4 + 6 = ___   6 + 4 = ___

$$\begin{array}{r} 6 \\ +3 \\ \hline \end{array}$$

4.

3 + 5 = ___   2 + 2 = ___

$$\begin{array}{r} 3 \\ +5 \\ \hline \end{array}$$

5.

3 + 4 = ___   7 + 2 = ___

$$\begin{array}{r} 2 \\ +7 \\ \hline \end{array}$$

6.

5 + 0 = ___   0 + 4 = ___

$$\begin{array}{r} 0 \\ +5 \\ \hline \end{array}$$

© Harcourt

CW8   Challenge

Name _____

Problem Solving • At the Store

Circle the two objects you can buy for 10¢ or less.
Write the addition sentence.

1.

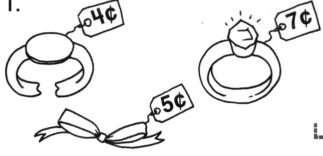

___4___ ¢ + ___5___ ¢ = ___9___ ¢

2.

_____ ¢ + _____ ¢ = _____ ¢

3.

_____ ¢ + _____ ¢ = _____ ¢

4.

_____ ¢ + _____ ¢ = _____ ¢

© Harcourt

Name _____

Good-bye Chickens!

Circle the chickens that go away.
Write numbers to finish each story.

1.

  __6__ chickens   __2__ go away   4 are left

2.

  _____ chickens   _____ go away   2 are left

3.

  _____ chickens   _____ goes away   I is left

4.

  _____ chickens   _____ go away   3 are left

CW 10   Challenge

© Harcourt

Name _____

Draw and Take Away

Draw a picture to show the subtraction sentence.
Write how many are left.

1.

$5 - 2 = \underline{3}$

2.

$4 - 3 = \underline{}$

3.

$3 - 2 = \underline{}$

4.

$6 - 4 = \underline{}$

5.

$5 - 3 = \underline{}$

6.

$2 - 1 = \underline{}$

© Harcourt

Challenge   CW 11

Make Up Subtraction Sentences

Cross out some in each row.
Complete the subtraction sentences.

1.  6 – 1 = 5

2.  ___ – ___ = ___

3.  ___ – ___ = ___

4.   ___ – ___ = ___

5. 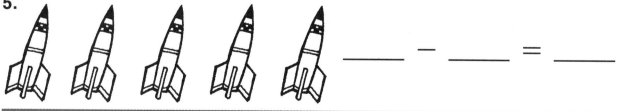 ___ – ___ = ___

6.   ___ – ___ = ___

© Harcourt

Fun in the Sun

Use the numbers to write 2 subtraction sentences.

1.

2   1   3

3 − 2 = 1   3 − 1 = 2

2.

2   5   3

___ − ___ = ___   ___ − ___ = ___

3.

 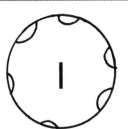 

4   1   3

___ − ___ = ___   ___ − ___ = ___

4.

2   4   6

___ − ___ = ___   ___ − ___ = ___

© Harcourt

Name _____

LESSON 3.5

Fact Flowers

Start with the number in the center.
Subtract. Write each difference.

CW 14   Challenge

Tree Time!

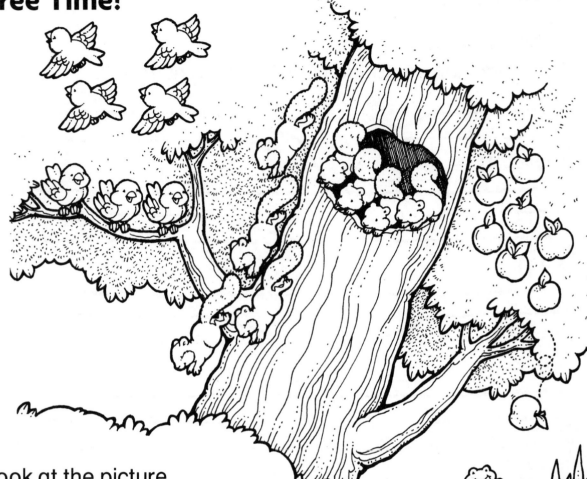

Look at the picture.
Complete the number sentence.

1. $\underline{7} - \underline{4} = \underline{3}$

2. $\underline{\hspace{1cm}} - \underline{\hspace{1cm}} = \underline{\hspace{1cm}}$

3. $\underline{\hspace{1cm}} - \underline{\hspace{1cm}} = \underline{\hspace{1cm}}$

4. 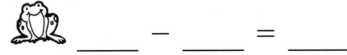 $\underline{\hspace{1cm}} - \underline{\hspace{1cm}} = \underline{\hspace{1cm}}$

© Harcourt

Mirror Math

Find the difference.
Write an addition sentence with the same numbers.

1.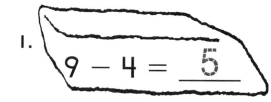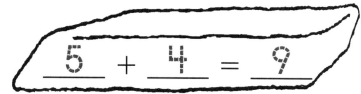
9 – 4 = __5__   __5__ + __4__ = __9__

2.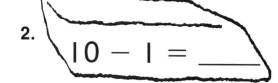
10 – 1 = ____   ____ + ____ = ____

3.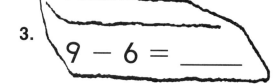
9 – 6 = ____   ____ + ____ = ____

4.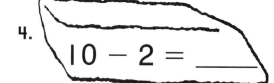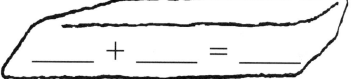
10 – 2 = ____   ____ + ____ = ____

5.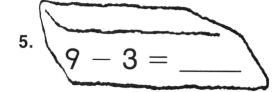
9 – 3 = ____   ____ + ____ = ____

6. How can you use an addition sentence
to check a subtraction sentence?

_____

_____

_____

_____

© Harcourt

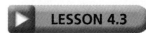

Find the Flags

Write the difference on the 🏳.

Then complete the fact on the ▽ that matches.

Use the key. Color the flags by the difference.

Color 1 | green |▷.   Color 6 | red |▷.

Color 5 | blue |▷.   Color 7 | yellow |▷.

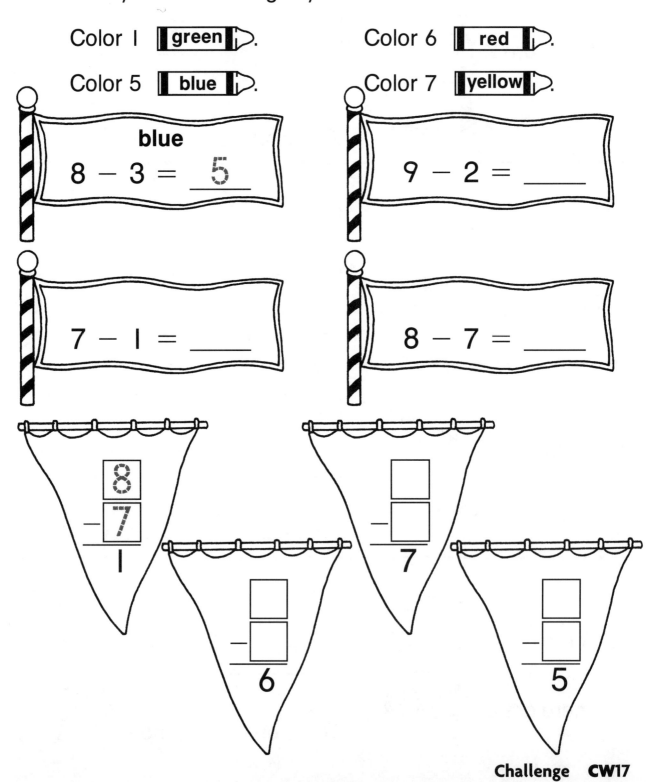

blue

$8 - 3 = \underline{5}$

$7 - 1 = \underline{}$

$9 - 2 = \underline{}$

$8 - 7 = \underline{}$

© Harcourt

Name _____

Subtract to Compare

How many more are there?
Complete the number sentence to solve.

1. There are 7 .

There are 5 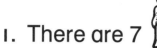.

$$7 - 5 = 2$$

There are __2__ more .

---

2. There are 9 .

There are 2 .

___ − ___ = ___

There are ___ more .

---

3. There are 10 .

There are 4 .

___ − ___ = ___

There are ___ more .

---

4. There are 8 .

There are 6 .

___ − ___ = ___

There are ___ more 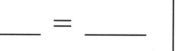.

© Harcourt

Name _____

Words and Pictures

Use the picture clues to write a subtraction story.
Write the subtraction sentence.
Solve.

1.

I have 5 erasers.
I put 2 in a box.
How many are left?

___5___ – ___2___ = ___3___ erasers left

2.

_____
_____
_____

_____ – _____ = _____ crayon on table

3.

_____
_____
_____

_____ – _____ = _____ cups spilled

© Harcourt

Count with Stories

Match the addition sentence
to the story. Find the sum.

1. Kara had 8 stickers.
   She found 2 more.
   How many stickers
   did she have in all?

   $9 + 1 =$ _____

2. Michael had 5 pens.
   He found 1 more.
   How many pens did
   he have in all?

   $8 + 2 = \underline{10}$

3. Luis read 5 books.
   He read 2 more.
   How many books did
   he read in all?

   $8 + 1 =$ _____

   $5 + 1 =$ _____

4. Maria completed 8
   puzzles. She did 1 more.
   How many puzzles did
   she do in all?

   $5 + 2 =$ _____

5. Anna drew 9 pictures.
   She drew 1 more.
   How many pictures did
   she draw in all?

© Harcourt

Name _____

Fishy Fun

Use the number line.
Count on to find the sum.
Then use the key.
Color the part by its sum.

7 | green
8 | yellow
9 | pink
10 | blue

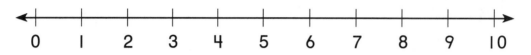

0 1 2 3 4 5 6 7 8 9 10

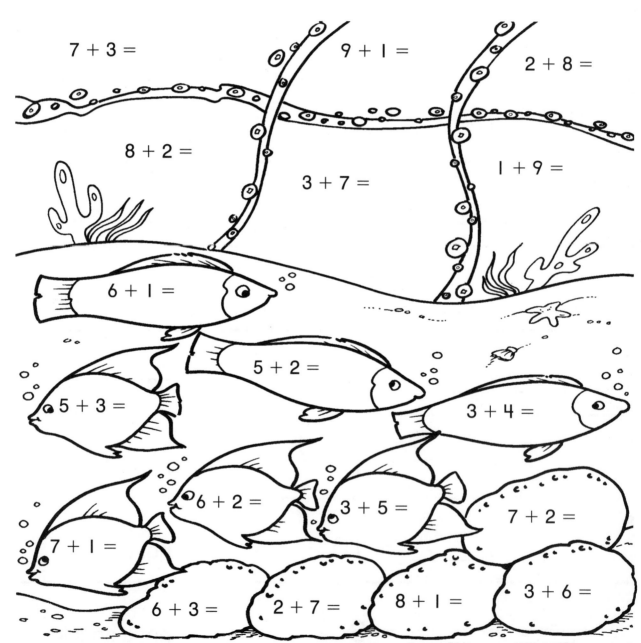

7 + 3 =

9 + 1 =

2 + 8 =

8 + 2 =

3 + 7 =

1 + 9 =

6 + 1 =

5 + 2 =

5 + 3 =

3 + 4 =

6 + 2 =

3 + 5 =

7 + 2 =

7 + 1 =

6 + 3 =

2 + 7 =

8 + 1 =

3 + 6 =

© Harcourt

Challenge CW21

What Was Doubled?

Complete the doubles fact for the sum.
Circle **not a double** if there is no
doubles fact for that sum.

1.

   _3_ + _3_ = 6   not a double

___

2.

   ___ + ___ = 5   (not a double)

___

3.

   ___ + ___ = 4   not a double

___

4.

   ___ + ___ = 8   not a double

___

5.

   ___ + ___ = 7   not a double

___

6.

   ___ + ___ = 2   not a double

___

7.

   ___ + ___ = 9   not a double

___

8.

   ___ + ___ = 10   not a double

___

9.

   ___ + ___ = 3   not a double

© Harcourt

Addition Riddles

Draw a picture to solve the riddle.
Write an addition sentence to check.

1. 3 seals sleep on the beach.
   The same number sleep on the rocks.
   How many seals are sleeping?

   _____ + _____ = _____ seals

2. Sam is looking at 2 rocks.
   Each rock has 5 crabs on it.
   How many crabs does Sam see?

   _____ + _____ = _____ crabs

3. Betty counts 2 orange fish.
   She counts the same
   number of blue fish.
   How many fish does Betty count?

   _____ + _____ = _____ fish

4. There are 2 caves in the sea.
   Each cave has 4 clams in it.
   How many clams are there?

   _____ + _____ = _____ clams

© Harcourt

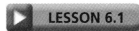

Name _____

Playground Addition

Count on 1, 2, or 3, or add
doubles to find the sum.
Then use the key.
Color the part by its sum.

6 | yellow
7 | green
8 | blue
10 | red

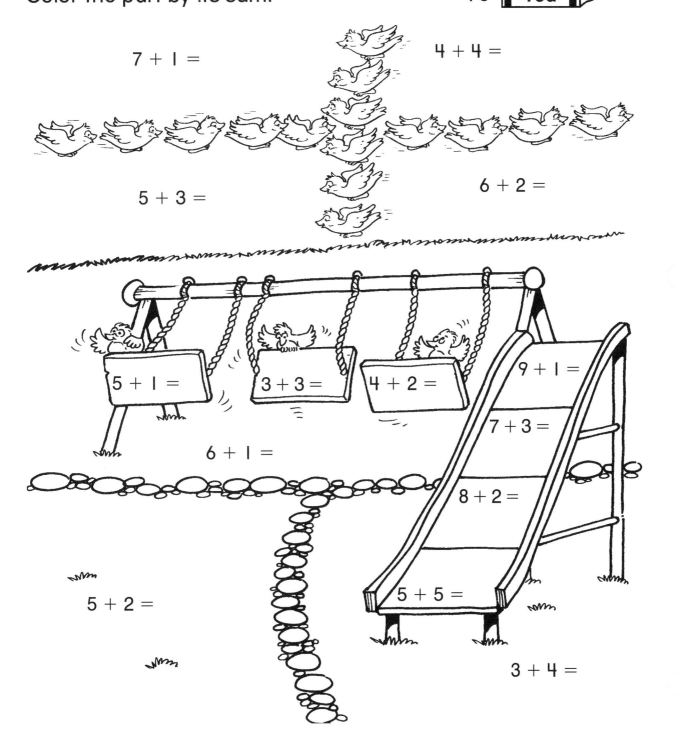

Some Sums

Write the sum. Change the order.
Write the new fact.

1.

$$6$$
$$+\ 2$$
$$\overline{\boxed{8}}$$

$$+\ \boxed{\begin{array}{c}2\\6\end{array}}$$
$$\overline{\boxed{8}}$$

2.

$$1 + 7 = \boxed{8}$$

$$\boxed{7} + \boxed{1} = \boxed{8}$$

3.

$$1$$
$$+\ 5$$
$$\overline{\boxed{}}$$

$$+\ \boxed{\begin{array}{c}\ \\ \ \end{array}}$$
$$\overline{\boxed{}}$$

4.

$$2 + 3 = \boxed{}$$

$$\boxed{} + \boxed{} = \boxed{}$$

5.

$$4$$
$$+\ 2$$
$$\overline{\boxed{}}$$

$$+\ \boxed{\begin{array}{c}\ \\ \ \end{array}}$$
$$\overline{\boxed{}}$$

6.

$$3 + 5 = \boxed{}$$

$$\boxed{} + \boxed{} = \boxed{}$$

7.

$$2$$
$$+\ 6$$
$$\overline{\boxed{}}$$

$$+\ \boxed{\begin{array}{c}\ \\ \ \end{array}}$$
$$\overline{\boxed{}}$$

8.

$$0 + 7 = \boxed{}$$

$$\boxed{} + \boxed{} = \boxed{}$$

© Harcourt

Some More Sums

Write ways to make 9.
Look for a pattern.

1. $0 + \boxed{9} = 9$

$\boxed{} + 8 = 9$

$2 + \boxed{} = 9$

$\boxed{} + 6 = 9$

$4 + \boxed{} = 9$

$5 + \boxed{} = 9$

$\boxed{} + 3 = 9$

$7 + \boxed{} = 9$

$\boxed{} + 1 = 9$

$9 + \boxed{} = 9$

What pattern do you see?

Write ways to make 10.
Look for a pattern.

2. $0 + \boxed{} = 10$

$1 + \boxed{} = 10$

$\boxed{} + 8 = 10$

$\boxed{} + 7 = 10$

$4 + \boxed{} = 10$

$\boxed{} + 5 = 10$

$6 + \boxed{} = 10$

$\boxed{} + 3 = 10$

$\boxed{} + 2 = 10$

$9 + \boxed{} = 10$

$10 + \boxed{} = 10$

What pattern do you see?

© Harcourt

Butterfly Tables

Complete the table.
Follow the rule.

1. Add 2

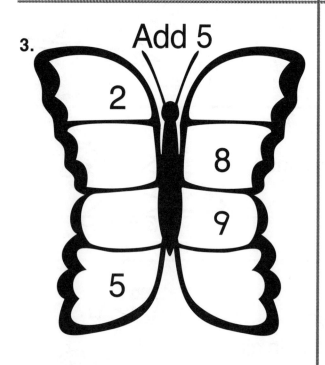

0
2
1
3
2
4
3
5

2. Add 6

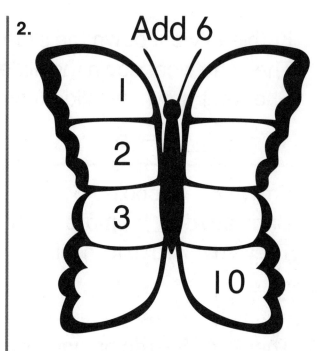

1
2
3
10

3. Add 5

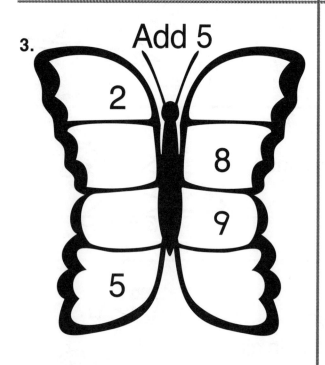

2
8
9
5

4. Add 4

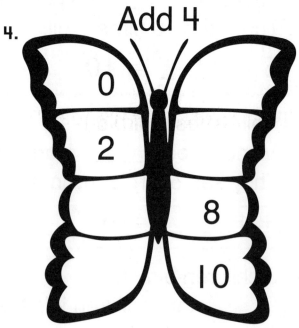

0
2
8
10

© Harcourt

What Is Missing?

Solve. Write the missing number.
Complete the number sentence.

1. Kathleen went down the slide 1 time.
   Then she went down the slide __5__ more times.
   She went down the slide 6 times in all.

   1 + __5__ = 6

2. Emily saw 3 rabbits.
   Brian saw _____ more rabbits.
   They saw 7 rabbits in all.

   3 + ____ = 7

3. There are 5 birds on one branch.
   There are _____ birds on another branch.
   There are 10 birds in all.

   5 + ____ = 10

4. Holly sees 4 airplanes.
   Manuel sees _____ more airplanes.
   They see 6 airplanes in all.

   4 + ____ = 6

5. 3 children play tag.
   _____ more children join them.
   There are 8 children playing tag in all.

   3 + ____ = 8

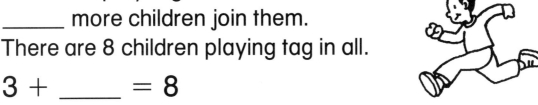

© Harcourt

Name _____

Count Back Number Pick

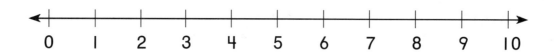

0   1   2   3   4   5   6   7   8   9   10

Pick a number.	Subtract.	Write the difference.
1. _9_	− 1	= _8_
2. ___	− 1	= ___
3. ___	− 2	= ___
4. ___	− 2	= ___
5. ___	− 1	= ___
6. ___	− 2	= ___
7. ___	− 2	= ___
8. ___	− 1	= ___

© Harcourt

Where Am I?

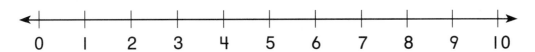

0   1   2   3   4   5   6   7   8   9   10

Use the number line. Solve.

1. I am at 4.
   I move left 3.
   Where am I? ____

2. I am at 7.
   I move right 3.
   Where am I? ____

3. I am at 3.
   I move right 1.
   Where am I? ____

4. I am at 5.
   I move left 2.
   Where am I? ____

5. I am at 8.
   I move right 2.
   Where am I? ____

6. I am at 6.
   I move left 1.
   Where am I? ____

7. I am at 10.
   I move left 3.
   Where am I? ____

8. I am at 2.
   I move left 2.
   Where am I? ____

9. I am at 9.
   I move left 3.
   Where am I? ____

10. I am at 5.
    I move right 3.
    Where am I? ____

© Harcourt

Add Some, Take Some

Use ● to model the problems. Then solve.

1. There are 5 markers
in the box.
Jon adds 2 markers.
Lindsay adds 1 marker.
How many markers are
in the box now?

_____ markers

There are 8 markers
in the box.
Jon takes 2 markers.
Lindsay takes 1 marker.
How many markers are
in the box now?

_____ markers

2. There are 3 crayons
on the table.
Ned adds 2 more crayons.
Bill adds 2 more crayons.
How many crayons are
on the table now?

_____ crayons

There are 7 crayons
on the table.
Ned takes 2 crayons.
Bill takes 2 crayons.
How many crayons are
on the table now?

_____ crayons

3. There are 4 stickers
on the sheet.
Michele adds 3 stickers.
Jordan adds 2 stickers
How many stickers are on
the sheet now?

_____ stickers

There are 9 stickers
on the sheet.
Michele takes 3 stickers.
Jordan takes 2 stickers
How many stickers are on
the sheet now?

_____ stickers

© Harcourt

Now You See It

Draw the hidden parts to solve the problem.

1. There are 2 dogs.
   From the side, you can
   see only 4 legs.
   How many legs are there in all?

   __8__ legs.

2. You can see 10 sneakers
   under the table.
   How many children are
   sitting at the table?

   _____ children.

3. There are 2 children roller-skating.
   From the side, you can see only
   4 wheels.
   How many wheels are there in all?

   _____ wheels.

4. There are 2 children riding tricycles.
   How many wheels are there in all?

   _____ wheels.

© Harcourt

CW32   Challenge

Name _____

Which Fact Am I?

Solve the riddle. Write the fact.

1. I am a **subtract zero** fact.
   My difference is 10.
   Which fact am I?

$$\underline{10} \; \bigcirc \; \underline{0} \; \bigcirc \; \underline{10}$$

2. I am a **count back 3** fact.
   Start with 7.
   Which fact am I?

___ ◯ ___ ◯ ___

3. I am a **subtract all** fact.
   Start with 6.
   Which fact am I?

___ ◯ ___ ◯ ___

4. I am a **count back 2** fact.
   My difference is 7.
   Which fact am I?

___ ◯ ___ ◯ ___

5. I am a **count back 3** fact.
   My difference is 5.
   Which fact am I?

___ ◯ ___ ◯ ___

6. I am a **subtract zero** fact.
   My difference is 1.
   Which fact am I?

___ ◯ ___ ◯ ___

7. I am a **count back 1** fact.
   My difference is 9.
   Which fact am I?

___ ◯ ___ ◯ ___

8. I am a **count back 2** fact.
   Start with 6.
   Which fact am I?

___ ◯ ___ ◯ ___

© Harcourt

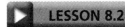

What's Missing?

Write the missing numbers.

1.

$10 - 8 = 5 - \underline{3}$

2.

$3 + 2 = 6 - \underline{}$

3.

$7 + 1 = \underline{} - 2$

4.

$5 + \underline{} = 10 - 2$

5.

$9 - 5 = 6 - \underline{}$

6.

$\underline{} - 3 = 5 + 1$

7.

$8 - 1 = 9 - \underline{}$

8.

$10 - 2 = 9 - \underline{}$

9.

$\underline{} + 1 = 10 - 6$

10.

$\underline{} - 5 = 10 - 10$

11.

$5 + \underline{} = 9 - 4$

12.

$\underline{} - 3 = 3 + 2$

13.

$10 - 3 = \underline{} + 5$

14.

$8 + \underline{} = 3 + 7$

15.

$\underline{} + 2 = 10 - \underline{}$

16.

$\underline{} - 3 = \underline{} + 1$

© Harcourt

What Goes In?

Follow the rule. Write the number that goes in.

1.

Subtract 2	
IN	OUT
4	2
	3
	4
	5

2.

Subtract 0	
IN	OUT
	6
	7
	8
	9

3.

Subtract 5	
IN	OUT
	5
	4
	3
	2

4.

Subtract 3	
IN	OUT
	2
	7
	3
	1

5.

Subtract 1	
IN	OUT
	0
	6
	9
	3

6.

Subtract 4	
IN	OUT
	0
	5
	2
	6

© Harcourt

Build the Fact Family

Use the numbers to write a fact family.

1. 5   2   7

$5 + 2 = 7$

___ + ___ = ___

___ − ___ = ___

___ − ___ = ___

2. 6   6   0

___ + ___ = ___

___ + ___ = ___

___ − ___ = ___

___ − ___ = ___

3. 2   8   10

___ + ___ = ___

___ + ___ = ___

___ − ___ = ___

___ − ___ = ___

4. 6   1   5

___ + ___ = ___

___ + ___ = ___

___ − ___ = ___

___ − ___ = ___

5. 1   9   10

___ + ___ = ___

___ + ___ = ___

___ − ___ = ___

___ − ___ = ___

6. 3   3   6

___ + ___ = ___

___ − ___ = ___

© Harcourt

CW36   Challenge

Supermarket Fun

Add and subtract to solve.
Write two number sentences.

1. Amy has 10¢.
   She buys 1 apple and 1 orange.
   How much money does she have left?

$$\underline{5} + \underline{4} = \underline{9} \qquad \underline{10} - \underline{9} = \underline{1}$$

2. Maya has 8¢
   She buys 2 bananas.
   How much money does she have left?

___ ◯ ___ ◯ ___   ___ ◯ ___ ◯ ___

3. Juan has 9¢.
   He buys 1 banana and 1 peach.
   How much money does he have left?

___ ◯ ___ ◯ ___   ___ ◯ ___ ◯ ___

4. Evan has 6¢.
   He buys 1 orange and 1 peach.
   How much money does he have left?

___ ◯ ___ ◯ ___   ___ ◯ ___ ◯ ___

© Harcourt

What Is My Label?

These shapes are sorted.

1. Write how each group is sorted.

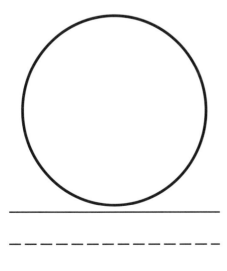   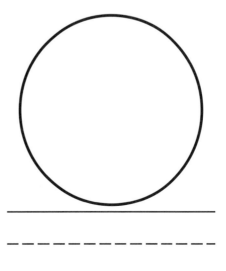

_____   _____

- - - - - - - - - - -   - - - - - - - - - - -

_____   _____

2. Sort the shapes in a different way.
   Draw each group. Write to tell how you sorted.

_____   _____

- - - - - - - - - - -   - - - - - - - - - - -

_____   _____

© Harcourt

Graph Clues

Use the clues below to make a graph.

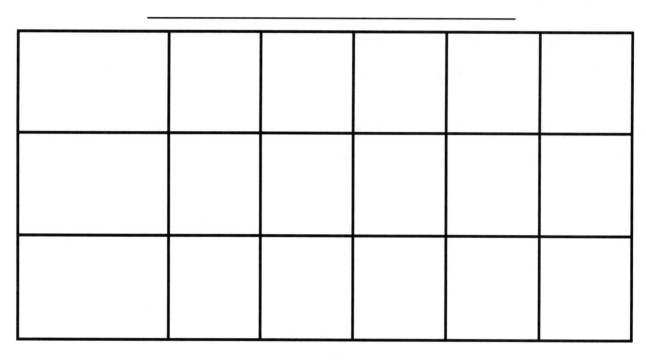

1. The graph is about favorite games.

2. The games are baseball, soccer, and football.

3. 3 people chose football.

4. 2 more people chose soccer than football.

5. 9 people were asked to choose.

Write two questions about your graph.
Give them to a friend to answer.

6. _____

_____

7. _____

© Harcourt

Picture Graph Riddles

1. Solve each riddle to find out how many children choose each kind of fruit.

 The number of children who choose apples is equal to 2 + 1.　　　　3

 The number of children who choose oranges is one more than the number of those who choose apples.　　　　———

 The number of children who choose bananas is one less than 6.　　　　———

2. Color the fruit below. Then fill in the picture graph. Draw and color the fruit to show how many children choose each kind.

Fruit We Like				

© Harcourt

The Marching Band

1. Sort the children. Complete the tally chart.
Draw tally marks to show how many
are in each group.

Instruments or Flags	
Instruments	||||
Flags	

2. Sort the children another way.

Write a question about one tally chart.
Have a classmate answer your question.

_____

_____

_____

© Harcourt

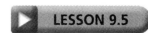
Roll a Number

1. Roll a number cube 10 times.
   Make a tally mark to show each number you roll.
   Write the total.

	Tally Marks	Total
1		
2		
3		
4		
5		
6		

2. Color the graph to match the tally marks.

	Numbers Rolled									
One										
Two										
Three										
Four										
Five										
Six										

    0   1   2   3   4   5   6   7   8   9   10

3. Which number did you roll the most times? _____

Graphing Sports

Ask your classmates which sport they like the best.
Have them choose from baseball, soccer, basketball,
and swimming.
Then use the information to make a bar graph.

Favorite Sports	
baseball	
soccer	
basketball	
swimming	

Use your graph to answer the questions.

1. How many children chose their favorite sport?

   _____

2. Which sport did the most children choose?

   _____

3. Which sport did the fewest children choose?

   _____

4. How many children chose baseball or basketball?

   _____

5. Write a question of your own about your graph.

   _____

   _____

   _____

© Harcourt

Across the Ages

Each child wrote his or her age on a card.
Use the cards to make a bar graph.

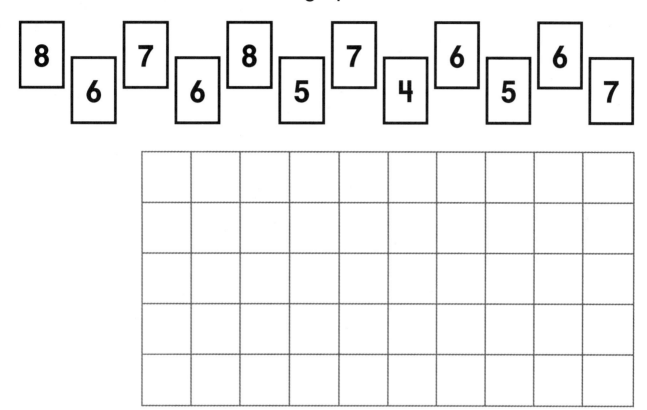

8   7   8   7   6   6
 6   6   5   4   5   7

Use your graph to answer the questions.

1. What age were the most children? _____ years

2. How old was the youngest child? _____ years

3. How many children were 8 years old? _____ children

4. What is the least number in the graph? _____

5. What is the greatest number in the graph? _____

6. What is the difference between the least and greatest numbers? _____

© Harcourt

Think About It

Read the clues. Write the number.

1. I have 1 ten.
   I have 0 ones.
   What number am I?

   _10_

2. I have 1 ten.
   I have 7 ones.
   What number am I?

   _____

3. I have 1 ten.
   I have 5 ones.
   What number am I?

   _____

4. I have 2 tens.
   I have 0 ones.
   What number am I?

   _____

5. I have 1 ten.
   I have 1 more than 5 ones.
   What number am I?

   _____

6. I have 1 ten.
   I have 2 more than 6 ones.
   What number am I?

   _____

7. I have 1 ten.
   I have 3 more than 1 one.
   What number am I?

   _____

8. I have 1 ten.
   I have 1 more than 0 ones.
   What number am I?

   _____

© Harcourt

Name _____

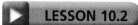

Circle Tens

How many objects are there? Circle tens to find out.
Write the numbers.

1.

$\dfrac{3}{\text{tens}}$ $\dfrac{30}{\text{moons}}$

2.

$\dfrac{}{\text{tens}}$ $\dfrac{}{\text{stars}}$

3.

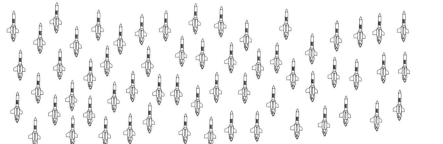

$\dfrac{}{\text{tens}}$ $\dfrac{}{\text{rockets}}$

4.

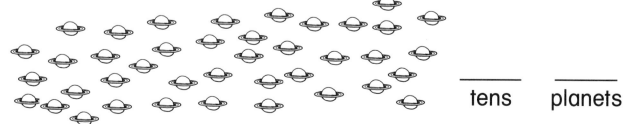

$\dfrac{}{\text{tens}}$ $\dfrac{}{\text{planets}}$

CW46 Challenge

© Harcourt

Books By Tens

Find the row of 24 books. Color the books red.
Find the row of 45 books. Color them blue.
Color the row of 17 books yellow.
Color the row of 36 books green.
Color the row of 52 books orange.

© Harcourt

Name _____

Sewing Circles

How many? Circle as many tens as you can.
Then count ones.

1.

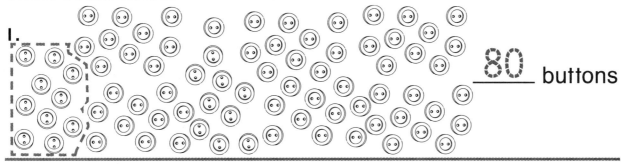

_____80_____ buttons

2.

_____ spools

3.

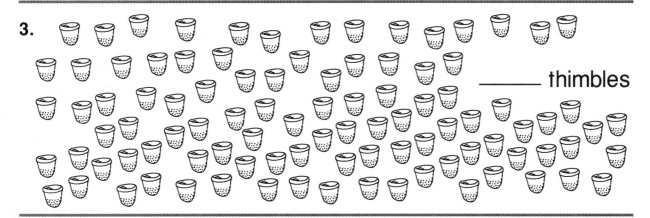

_____ thimbles

4.

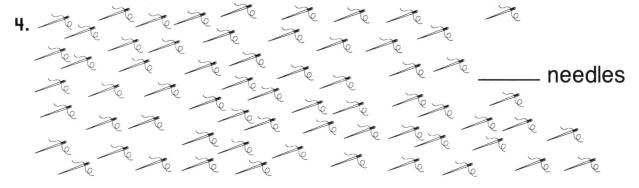

_____ needles

© Harcourt

CW48 Challenge

Pennies and Dimes

Use what you know
about pennies and dimes
to solve the problem.

10 pennies = 1 dime

---

1. Andy has 7 dimes.
   He finds 3 pennies.
   How much money
   does he have?

   $\underline{70}$ ¢ + $\underline{3}$ ¢ = $\underline{73}$ ¢

2. Kelli has 6 dimes.
   She finds 2 pennies.
   How much money
   does she have?

   ___¢ + ___¢ = ___¢

---

3. Ernie has 4 dimes.
   He finds 7 pennies.
   How much money
   does he have?

   ___¢ + ___¢ = ___¢

4. Cindy has 5 dimes.
   She finds 1 penny.
   How much money
   does she have?

   ___¢ + ___¢ = ___¢

---

5. Roxie has 3 dimes.
   She finds 8 pennies.
   How much money
   does she have?

   ___¢ + ___¢ = ___¢

6. Wayne has 2 dimes.
   He finds 6 pennies.
   How much money
   does he have?

   ___¢ + ___¢ = ___¢

© Harcourt

How Many Can Fit?

About how many more objects do you need to fill the shelf?
Circle the best estimate.

1.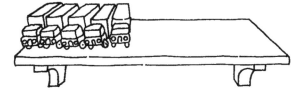

About how many more are needed?

about 5   about 15   about 25

2.

About how many more are needed?

about 5   about 10   about 15

3.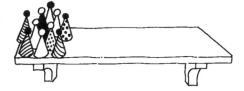

About how many more are needed?

about 10   about 20   about 30

4.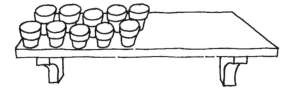

About how many more are needed?

about 5   about 10   about 20

© Harcourt

Name _____

Number Ride

1. Color each  that has a number greater than 30.

25   43   100   13

2. Color each ✈ that has a number greater than 60.

61   39   64   86

3. Color each 🚢 that has a number greater than 90.

96   55   100   89

4. Color each 🚚 that has a number greater than 50.

26   68   94   45

© Harcourt

Name _____

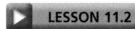

More or Less

Fill in numbers to make
the symbols correct.

1.

   _20_ > 15

2.

   ___ < 80

3.

   22 > ___

4.

   3 + 2 > ___

5.

   9 + 1 < ___

6.

   72 < ___

7.

   ___ > ___

8.

   3 + ___ > ___

9.

   ___ < ___

10.

   18 < ___

11.

   ___ < 4 + ___

12.

   ___ < 2

© Harcourt

What's My Symbol?

Write <, >, or = in the circles.

Color the boxes with < [red ▷ .

Color the boxes with = [blue ▷ .

Color the boxes with > [green ▷ .

86 ⟩ 62	85 ◯ 95	4 + 3 ◯ 5
15 ◯ 23	5 + 5 ◯ 6 + 4	6 ◯ 5 + 3
3 + 0 ◯ 2 + 1	25 ◯ 52	19 ◯ 9

Name _____

Riddles for Before, After, Between

Read the riddle. Write the number.

1. I am a number
between 40 and 42.
What number am I?

    __41__

2. I am a number
that comes after 29
and before 31.
What number am I?

    _____

3. I am a number
between 16 and 18.
What number am I?

    _____

4. I am a number
that comes after 65
and before 67.
What number am I?

    _____

5. We are numbers
that come after 23
and before 27.
What numbers are we?

    ____ , ____ , ____

6. We are numbers
that come after 44
and before 48.
What numbers are we?

    ____ , ____ , ____

7. We are numbers
that come after 28
and before 32.
What numbers are we?

    ____ , ____ , ____

8. We are numbers
that come after 50
and before 54.
What numbers are we?

    ____ , ____ , ____

© Harcourt

Blast Off

Help each rocket count down.
Write the missing numbers.

1.

20
19
___
17
___
14
___

2.

25
___
23
21
___
___
18

3.

___
16
15
___
13
___
11
___
9

4.

8
___
___
___
___
___
0

© Harcourt

More Money, Less Money

Use the model ▭▭▭▭▭▭ ▱ .
Find 10 more or 10 less.
Write the numbers.

1. Joy has 80¢.
   Ray has 10¢ less than Joy.
   Tony has 10¢ less than Ray.
   How much money does Tony have?

   _____¢

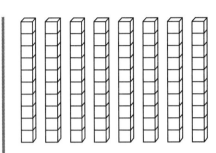

2. Art has 35¢.
   Ray has 10¢ more than Art.
   Lana has 10¢ more than Ray.
   How much money does Lana have?

   _____¢

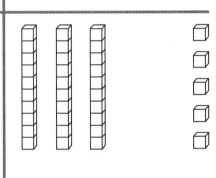

3. Steve has 22¢.
   Al has 10¢ less than Steve.
   Mike has 10¢ less than Al.
   How much money does Mike have?

   _____¢

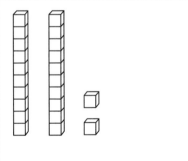

4. Jesse has 11¢.
   Greg has 10¢ more than Jesse.
   Martin has 10¢ more than Greg.
   How much money does Martin have?

   _____¢

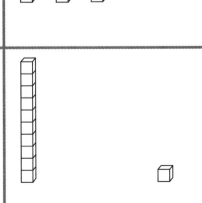

© Harcourt

Name _____

Count with Bees

Cut and paste. Count by twos, fives, or tens
to match the 🐝 to the 🌸.

1.

62 64 66

2.

80   100

3.

12   16

4.

40   50

5.

58   78

6.

25   35

| 14 | 30 | 64 | 45 | 68 | 90 |

© Harcourt

Coloring Patterns

1	2	3	4	5	6	7	8	9	10
11	12	13	14	15	16	17	18	19	20
21	22	23	24	25	26	27	28	29	30
31	32	33	34	35	36	37	38	39	40
41	42	43	44	45	46	47	48	49	50
51	52	53	54	55	56	57	58	59	60
61	62	63	64	65	66	67	68	69	70
71	72	73	74	75	76	77	78	79	80
81	82	83	84	85	86	87	88	89	90
91	92	93	94	95	96	97	98	99	100

1. Count by twos. Color the twos | red |▷.

2. Count by fives. Color the fives | blue |▷.

3. Color the numbers that are less than 31 | green |▷.

4. Which 3 numbers were colored | red |▷,
   | blue |▷, and | green |▷?

   _____ , _____ , _____

© Harcourt

Name _____

Number Scramble

Write the numbers in order by tens.

1.

23 | 3 | 53 | 33 | 63 | 43 | 83 | 13 | 73

__3__ , ____ , ____ , ____ , ____ , ____ , ____ , ____ , ____

2.

49 | 19 | 69 | 39 | 9 | 29 | 79 | 59 | 89

__9__ , ____ , ____ , ____ , ____ , ____ , ____ , ____ , ____

3.
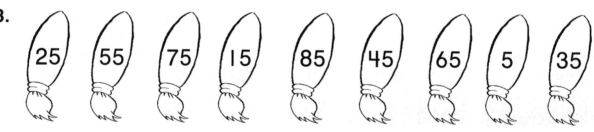

25 | 55 | 75 | 15 | 85 | 45 | 65 | 5 | 35

____ , ____ , ____ , ____ , ____ , ____ , ____ , ____ , ____

4.

70 | 30 | 100 | 80 | 50 | 40 | 90 | 60 | 20

____ , ____ , ____ , ____ , ____ , ____ , ____ , ____ , ____

© Harcourt

Challenge **CW59**

Odd and Even Riddles

Solve each riddle.

1. We are odd numbers.
   We are less than 10,
   but greater than 3.
   What numbers are we?

   _5_ , _7_ , _9_

2. We are even numbers.
   We are less than 13,
   but greater than 8.
   What numbers are we?

   ____ , ____

3. We are odd numbers.
   We are less than 40,
   but greater than 36.
   What numbers are we?

   ____ , ____

4. We are even numbers.
   We are less than 20,
   but greater than 12.
   What numbers are we?

   ____ , ____ , ____

5. List the odd numbers that are less than 20.

   _1_ , ____ , ____ , ____ , ____ , ____ , ____ , ____ , ____ , ____

6. Count by fives to 20. Write the numbers.

   ____ , ____ , ____ , ____

7. What numbers are on both lists? Write them.

   ____ , ____

© Harcourt

Name _____

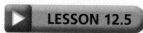

Next in Line

Find the pattern.
Write the next 3 numbers.

1. 2, 4, 6, 8, 10, <u>12</u>, <u>14</u>, <u>16</u>

2. 5, 10, 15, 20, 25, ____, ____, ____

3. 10, 20, 30, 40, 50, ____, ____, ____

4. 13, 15, 17, 19, 21, ____, ____, ____

5. 30, 40, 50, 60, 70, ____, ____, ____

6. 20, 25, 30, 35, 40, ____, ____, ____

7. 35, 40, 45, 50, 55, ____, ____, ____

8. 44, 46, 48, 50, 52, ____, ____, ____

9. 70, 80, 90, 100, 110, ____, ____, ____

10. 10, 20, 25, 30, 40, 45, ____, ____, ____

© Harcourt

Can You Place Me?

Write a word from the box to answer the problem.

second	fourth	sixth	tenth

1. Amy is first in line.
   Jack is third in line.
   Paul is standing
   between them.
   In which place is Paul?

2. Katie was third in line.
   She left the line.
   Matt was fifth in line.
   In which place is
   Matt now?

   _____

   _____

3. There are 10 children in
   line. Tasha is the next to
   the last in line. Rico is
   standing behind her.
   In which place is Rico?

   _____

   _____

4. Allen is fourth in line.
   Callie is next in line.
   Then comes Emma.
   In which place is Emma?

   _____

   _____

© Harcourt

Name _____

 LESSON 13.1

Count On with Arrows

Follow the rule to count on.

⟶ means **count on 1.** ⇢ means **count on 2.**

∿→ means **count on 3.**

1. 7 ∿→ _10_

2. 6 ∿→ ____

3. 10 ⇢ ____

4. 8 ⟶ ____

5. 6 ⟶ ____

6. 4 ⇢ ____

Find the starting number.

7. _9_ ⟶ 10

8. ____ ∿→ 12

9. ____ ⟶ 3

10. ____ ⇢ 7

11. ____ ∿→ 9

12. ____ ⇢ 11

Name _____

Mental Math

Solve the problem.

1. Tim picked 1 apple.
   Sally gave him 1 more.
   How many apples did
   he have in all?

    ___2___ apples

2. Tracy had 2 dresses.
   Her father made her
   3 more. How many dresses
   did she have in all?

    _____ dresses

3. Jim saw 5 baby birds.
   Then he saw 4 more.
   How many birds did he
   see in all?

    _____ birds

4. Matt found 6 eggs.
   His sister found the
   same number.
   How many eggs did
   they find in all?

    _____ eggs

5. Mike ate 3 plums.
   Morgan ate the same
   number of plums.
   How many plums did
   they eat in all?

    _____ plums

6. Karen wrapped 5 presents.
   Judy wrapped one more
   than Karen.
   How many presents
   did they wrap in all?

    _____ presents

© Harcourt

Name _____

At the Store

Add the prices to solve.

1. Trent has 12¢. He buys three objects.
Circle what he buys.

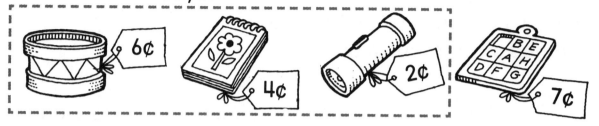

2. Iris has 8¢. She buys three objects.
Circle what she buys.

3. Abe has 11¢. He buys three objects.
Circle what he buys.

4. Jeannie has 9¢. She buys three objects.
Circle what she buys.

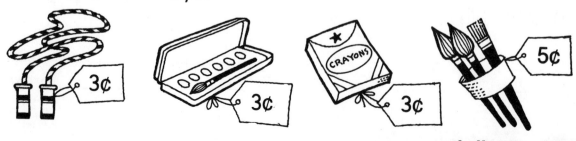

© Harcourt

Three Addends to Solve

Write a number sentence. Solve.

1. Mona ate 2 grapes. Rick ate the same number of grapes. Lee ate one more grape than Mona did. How many grapes did they eat in all?

   __2__ + __2__ + __3__ = __7__   __7__ grapes

2. Laina scored 5 goals. Bob scored 4 goals. Betty scored 3 goals. How many goals did they score in all?

   _____ + _____ + _____ = _____   _____ goals

3. Kate has one pet. Bill has one more than Kate. Artie has one more pet than Bill. How many pets do they have in all?

   _____ + _____ + _____ = _____   _____ pets

4. Susan has 3 crayons. Pat has 2 crayons. Anna has 2 more crayons than Pat. How many crayons do they have in all?

   _____ + _____ + _____ = _____   _____ crayons

© Harcourt

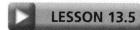

What Number Is Missing?

Fill in the missing number.

1.
```
   5
 -[3]
 ----
   2
```

2.
```
   9
 -[ ]
 ----
   8
```

3.
```
   3
 -[ ]
 ----
   0
```

4.
```
  10
 -[ ]
 ----
   7
```

5.
```
   2
 -[ ]
 ----
   0
```

6.
```
   4
 -[ ]
 ----
   3
```

7.
```
  10
 -[ ]
 ----
   8
```

8.
```
   2
 -[ ]
 ----
   1
```

9.
```
   6
 -[ ]
 ----
   3
```

10.
```
   1
 -[ ]
 ----
   0
```

11.
```
   3
 -[ ]
 ----
   1
```

12.
```
   9
 -[ ]
 ----
   6
```

© Harcourt

Name _____

Subtract to Compare

Write a number sentence. Subtract to compare.

1. Luis read 9 books. Tony read 6 books. How many more books did Luis read than Tony?

$$\underline{9} - \underline{6} = \underline{3}$$
more

2. Jennifer ate 12 grapes. Alice ate 4 grapes. How many more grapes did Jennifer eat than Alice?

$$\underline{} - \underline{} = \underline{}$$
more

3. Mona scored 3 goals. Ella scored 7 goals. How many more goals did Ella score than Mona?

$$\underline{} - \underline{} = \underline{}$$
more

4. Rob has 8 trophies. Sam has 11 trophies. How many more trophies does Sam have than Rob?

$$\underline{} - \underline{} = \underline{}$$
more

5. Sara has 5 puzzles. Kyle has 6 puzzles. How many more puzzles does Kyle have than Sara?

$$\underline{} - \underline{} = \underline{}$$
more

© Harcourt

CW68 Challenge

Build the Related Facts

Use the numbers to write an addition fact.
Then write the related subtraction fact.

1. 5, 3, 2   __3__ + __2__ = __5__   __5__ – __2__ = __3__

2. 1, 12, 11   _____ + _____ = _____   _____ – _____ = _____

3. 6, 2, 8   _____ + _____ = _____   _____ – _____ = _____

4. 7, 5, 12   _____ + _____ = _____   _____ – _____ = _____

5. 3, 9, 6   _____ + _____ = _____   _____ – _____ = _____

6. 4, 1, 3   _____ + _____ = _____   _____ – _____ = _____

7. 10, 6, 4   _____ + _____ = _____   _____ – _____ = _____

© Harcourt

Name _____

Flower Families

- Use these numbers. Pick three that can be used to write a fact family.
- Write the numbers in the flowers.
- Write the number sentences.

1.

$$2 + 3 = 5$$
$$3 + 2 = 5$$
$$5 - 3 = 2$$
$$5 - 2 = 3$$

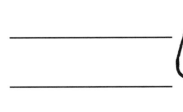

2.

3.

4.

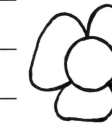

© Harcourt

Number Circles

Look at each row of circles.
Cross out a number in one circle so that all
the circles in the row have the same sum.

1.

What is the sum of the numbers in each circle?

9

2.

What is the sum of the numbers in each circle?

_____

3.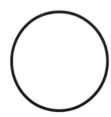

What is the sum of the numbers in each circle?

_____

4.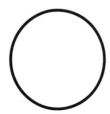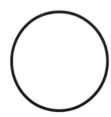

What is the sum of the numbers in each circle?

_____

Write your own problem. Then solve it.

5. ◯ ◯ ◯

What is the sum of the numbers in each circle?

_____

© Harcourt

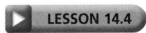

Picnic Pictures

Look at the pictures.
Write the two missing numbers.

1.

$\boxed{2} + 4 = \underline{6}$ sunglasses

2.

$\boxed{} + \boxed{} = 8$ picnic baskets

3.

$8 + \boxed{} = \boxed{}$ bottles

4.

$\boxed{} + 6 = \boxed{}$ apples

5.

$\boxed{} + \boxed{} = 12$ ants

© Harcourt

Addition and Subtraction Picnic

Choose a way to solve each problem.
Make a model 🎲.
Draw a picture ▭▷.
Write a number sentence ✏️.

1. Ellen has 7 plates. Henry takes 1. Hannah takes 1. How many plates does Ellen have left? ___5___ plates	🎲🎲🎲🎲 🎲🎲🎲 7 − 2 = 5
2. Jesse carries 3 baskets. Dave carries 2 baskets. Sara carries 1 basket. How many baskets do they carry in all? _____ baskets	
3. There are 5 sandwiches. Glen eats 2 sandwiches. Reggie eats 1 sandwich. How many sandwiches are left? _____ sandwiches	
4. Trent has 5 rocks. He finds 2 more rocks. Then he finds 1 more rock. How many rocks does Trent have now? _____ rocks	

© Harcourt

Sort for a Prize

Find out how the solids were sorted.
Write a letter on the prize ribbon.
Use each letter only one time.

A. They can roll.
B. They can slide but not roll.
C. They can stack and slide.

© Harcourt

Name _____

How Many Faces and Corners?

Circle the answers.
Use solids to check your answers.

Solid Figure	How Many Faces?	How Many Corners?
1. 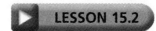	0 1 4	0 1 4
2.	1 2 6	0 1 2
3.	4 6 8	4 6 8
4.	0 2 4	0 2 4
5.	6 7 8	6 7 8
6.	4 5 6	4 5 6

© Harcourt

Challenge   CW75

Name _____

Plane Shapes

Color each square ▮ **red** ▷. Color each circle ▮ **blue** ▷.
Color each triangle ▮ **green** ▷. Color each rectangle ▮ **yellow** ▷.

I.

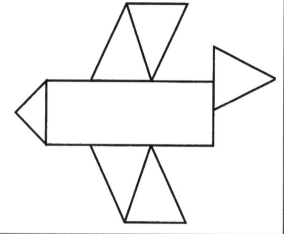

2.

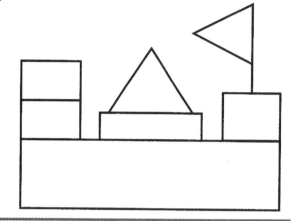

3.

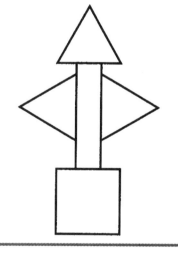

4.

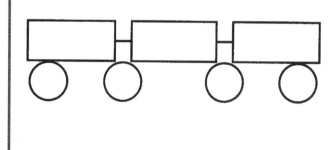

5.

6.

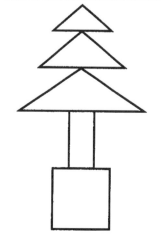

© Harcourt

Sides and Corners

Read the riddle.
Draw the answer.

1. I have 8 sides.
   I have 8 corners.
   I am the shape of a
   stop sign.

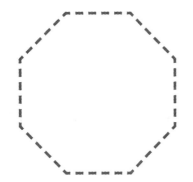

2. I have 5 sides.
   I have 5 corners.
   I look like the shape
   of a house.

Draw a picture to show each.

3. A shape with
   3 sides and 3 corners.

4. A shape with 4 sides and
   3 corners.

© Harcourt

Name _____

How Many Ways Can You Make It?

Use △ and ◇ .

Find four ways to make a ⬡ .

Trace the shapes to show your answers on this page.

1.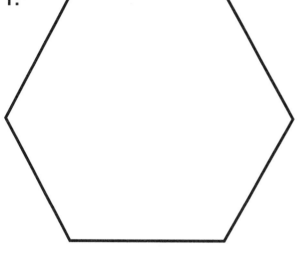

2.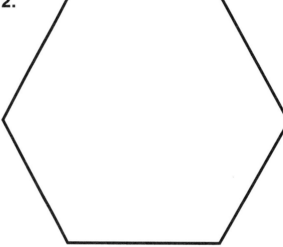

3.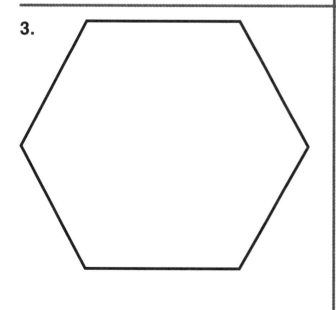

4.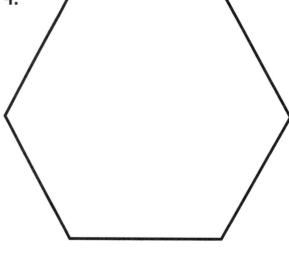

© Harcourt

Name _____

Odd Shape Out

Decide if each figure is open or closed.
Circle the figure that does not belong.

1.

2.

 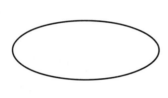  

3.

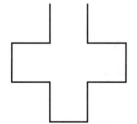 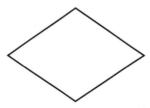 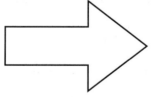 

4. C S D H

© Harcourt

Problem Solving Skill • Use a Picture

Where are you?
Follow the directions.

1. Color the animal yellow.
   You are to the left of the giraffe.
   You are behind the bear.

2. Color the animal brown .
   You are in front of the tiger and the zebra.
   You are to the left of the zoo sign.

3. Start at the zoo sign. Draw a path to the gift shop.
   Go behind the bear, to the left of the zebra,
   and in front of the tiger.

CW80   Challenge

© Harcourt

Secret Code

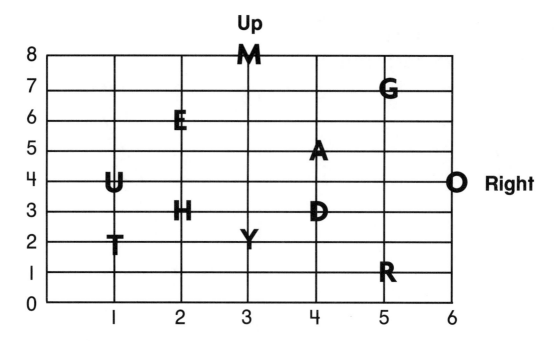

Up

Right

Start at 0. Go to the right and then up.
Write the letter. What do the words say?

Y	O	U				
3, 2	6, 4	1, 4		4, 5	5, 1	2, 6

5, 7	6, 4	6, 4	4, 3	4, 5	1, 2

3, 8	4, 5	1, 2	2, 3

© Harcourt

Make a Match

Draw the missing part.
Make the two parts match.

1.

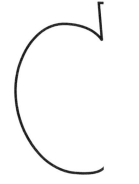

2.

3.

4.

5.

6.

© Harcourt

Draw It Right

Draw a slide or turn.
Draw the dot where it belongs.

1. Draw a slide.

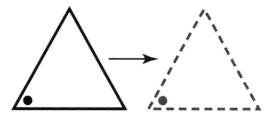

2. Draw a turn.

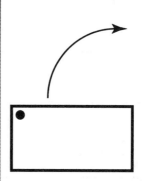

3. Draw a turn.

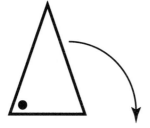

4. Draw a slide.

5. Draw a turn.

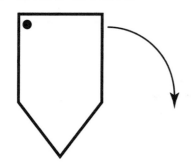

6. Draw a turn.

© Harcourt

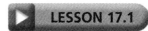

Follow the Pattern

Draw the shape to continue the pattern.

1.

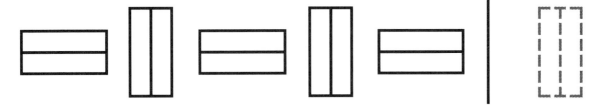

2.

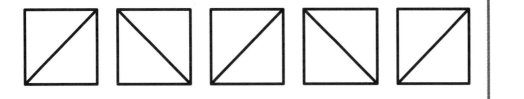

3.

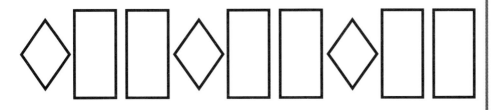

4.

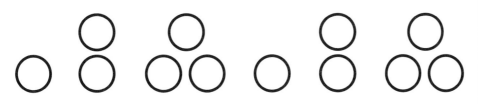

5.

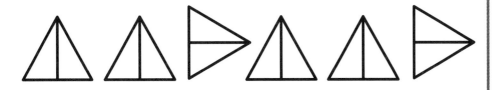

© Harcourt

Create Patterns

Use △ and ○.
Make up your own pattern for each row.
Circle the pattern unit.

1.
_____ _____ _____

2.
_____ _____ _____

3.
_____ _____ _____

4.
_____ _____ _____

© Harcourt

Make Your Own Patterns

Use the shapes to make your own pattern.

1.

2.

3.

4.

5.

CW86   Challenge

© Harcourt

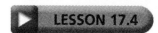

Pattern Path

Follow the path.
Cross out the mistakes in the pattern.
Paste new shapes to show the pattern the correct way.

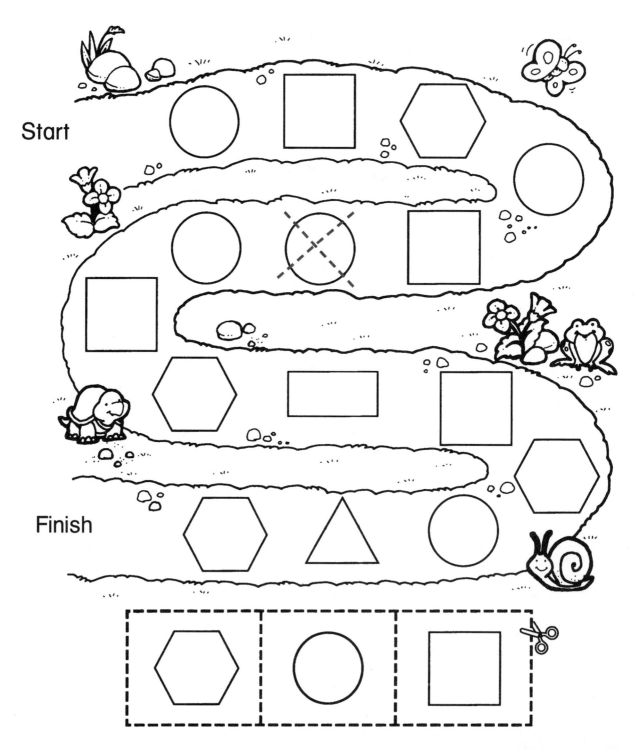

© Harcourt

Name _____

Missing Shapes

Draw the missing shapes or letters.

I.

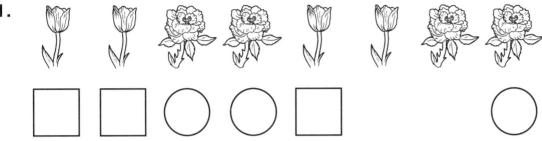

2. **A** **B** **B** **A** **A** **B** **B** **A**

3.

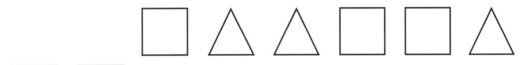

A ___ B A ___ ___ ___ A A ___

4.

A B C A ___ ___ ___ B C

© Harcourt

CW88   Challenge

Doubles Plus Two

Write the sum for the doubles problem.
Complete the doubles plus one problem.
Complete the doubles plus two problem.

1.

6	6	6
+ 6	+ 7	+ 8
12	13	14

2.

8	8	8
+ 8	+ ☐	+ ☐
☐	☐	☐

3.

5	5	5
+ 5	+ ☐	+ ☐
☐	☐	☐

4.

7	7	7
+ 7	+ ☐	+ ☐
☐	☐	☐

5.

4	4	4
+ 4	+ ☐	+ ☐
☐	☐	☐

6.

3	3	3
+ 3	+ ☐	+ ☐
☐	☐	☐

7.

2	2	2
+ 2	+ ☐	+ ☐
☐	☐	☐

8.

1	1	1
+ 1	+ ☐	+ ☐
☐	☐	☐

© Harcourt

Name _____

Name _____

LESSON 18.2

Ten and What?

Draw the missing 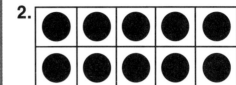.
Write the missing number.

1.
$$\begin{array}{r} 10 \\ +\ 4 \\ \hline 14 \end{array}$$

2.
$$\begin{array}{r} 10 \\ + \\ \hline 17 \end{array}$$

3.
$$\begin{array}{r} 10 \\ + \\ \hline 16 \end{array}$$

4.
$$\begin{array}{r} +\ 5 \\ \hline 15 \end{array}$$

5.
$$\begin{array}{r} 10 \\ + \\ \hline 12 \end{array}$$

6.
$$\begin{array}{r} 10 \\ + \\ \hline 20 \end{array}$$

7.
$$\begin{array}{r} 10 \\ + \\ \hline 11 \end{array}$$

8.
$$\begin{array}{r} 10 \\ + \\ \hline 18 \end{array}$$

© Harcourt

CW90   Challenge

Name _____

Make Dimes

Use mental math to find the sum.
Write the sum as a dime and pennies.

1. 9¢ + 6¢ = __1__ dime and __5__ pennies

2. 9¢ + 8¢ = ____ dime and ____ pennies

3. 9¢ + 2¢ = ____ dime and ____ penny

4. 9¢ + 5¢ = ____ dime and ____ pennies

5. 9¢ + 3¢ = ____ dime and ____ pennies

6. 9¢ + 9¢ = ____ dime and ____ pennies

7. 4¢ + 9¢ = ____ dime and ____ pennies

8. 7¢ + 9¢ = ____ dime and ____ pennies

9. 1¢ + 9¢ = ____ dime and ____ pennies

10. 9¢ + 10¢ = ____ dime and ____ pennies

© Harcourt

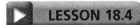

Gone Fishing

Draw a line from two fish to a bowl.
Together, the two fish must weigh the
number of pounds on the bowl.

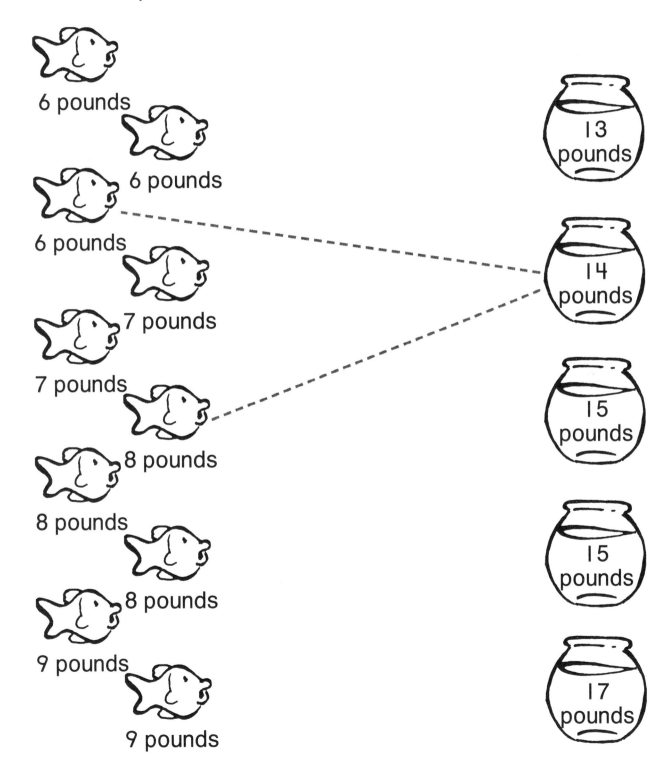

6 pounds

6 pounds

6 pounds

7 pounds

7 pounds

8 pounds

8 pounds

8 pounds

9 pounds

9 pounds

13 pounds

14 pounds

15 pounds

15 pounds

17 pounds

© Harcourt

Add Four Numbers

Write the numbers. Circle two that
make a ten or a double. Then add.

1.
```
  3
 (6)
 (4)
+ 2
 15
```

2. _____
_____
_____
+ _____

3. _____
_____
_____
+ _____

4. _____
_____
_____
+ _____

5. _____
_____
_____
+ _____

6. _____
_____
_____
+ _____

7. _____
_____
_____
+ _____

8. _____
_____
_____
+ _____

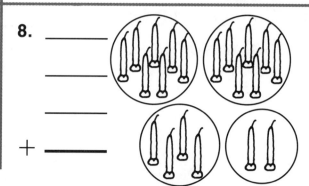

© Harcourt

Name _____

LESSON 18.6

Empty Tables

Fill in the numbers missing from the table. Use the clues.

1. The children saw 6 ladybugs.
2. They saw 2 more ladybugs than bees.
3. They saw 1 fewer ant than bees.
4. They saw 8 bugs that were not ladybugs.

Bugs in the Garden		
ant		
butterfly		
ladybug		
bee		

5. The children saw 3 roses.
6. They saw 1 fewer iris than roses.
7. They saw 3 more tulips than irises.
8. They saw 12 flowers that were not tulips.

Flowers in the Garden		
iris		
tulip		
rose		
daisy		

© Harcourt

CW94 Challenge

Name _____

14 Marks the Spot

Solve the subtraction problems. Use the number line to help.

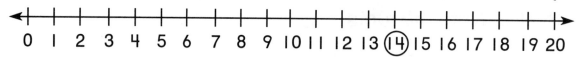

If the answer is greater than 14, color the box red.
If the answer is less than 14, color the box green.

17 − 1	13 − 1	19 − 3	13 − 3	20 − 3
18 − 2	12 − 2	17 − 2	11 − 1	18 − 1
20 − 1	10 − 2	19 − 2	18 − 3	19 − 1
16 − 1	11 − 2	12 − 1	13 − 2	20 − 2
19 − 1	10 − 1	11 − 3	12 − 3	17 − 2

© Harcourt

Challenge   CW95

Name _____

Make Doubles Fact Families

Circle the numbers that make a doubles
fact family. Write the facts.

1. 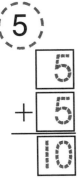 7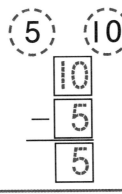

2. 3   4   3   6

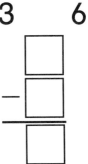

3. 6   9   6   12

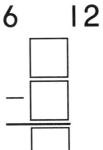   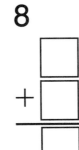

4. 8   14   8   16

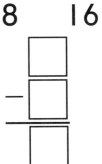

5. 7   5   7   14

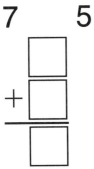   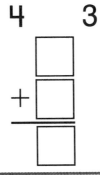

6. 4   3   4   8

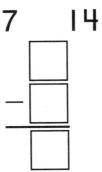   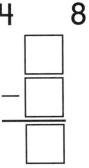

7. 9   8   9   18

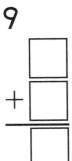   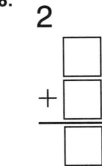

8. 2   6   2   4

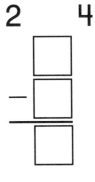

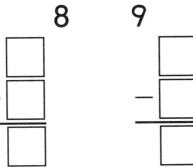

© Harcourt

Name _____

Number Families

Use the numbers to write an addition sentence.
Then write two related subtraction sentences.

1.

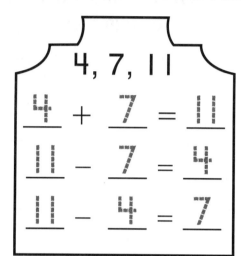

4, 7, 11

$$\underline{4} + \underline{7} = \underline{11}$$
$$\underline{11} - \underline{7} = \underline{4}$$
$$\underline{11} - \underline{4} = \underline{7}$$

2.

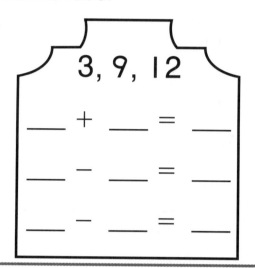

3, 9, 12

$$\underline{} + \underline{} = \underline{}$$
$$\underline{} - \underline{} = \underline{}$$
$$\underline{} - \underline{} = \underline{}$$

3.

5, 8, 13

$$\underline{} + \underline{} = \underline{}$$
$$\underline{} - \underline{} = \underline{}$$
$$\underline{} - \underline{} = \underline{}$$

4.

7, 9, 16

$$\underline{} + \underline{} = \underline{}$$
$$\underline{} - \underline{} = \underline{}$$
$$\underline{} - \underline{} = \underline{}$$

5.

6, 8, 14

$$\underline{} + \underline{} = \underline{}$$
$$\underline{} - \underline{} = \underline{}$$
$$\underline{} - \underline{} = \underline{}$$

6.

4, 6, 10

$$\underline{} + \underline{} = \underline{}$$
$$\underline{} - \underline{} = \underline{}$$
$$\underline{} - \underline{} = \underline{}$$

© Harcourt

Name _____

Garden Math

Circle the problem closest
to the estimate.

1. about 5	$10 + 6$ $5 + 5$ $(\widetilde{10 - 6})$
2. about 20 	$9 + 9$ $9 + 3$ $9 + 1$
3. about 10 	$10 - 6$ $9 + 7$ $2 + 9$
4. about 15 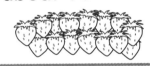	$2 + 4$ $7 + 7$ $12 - 3$
5. about 20 	$10 + 4$ $11 + 8$ $12 - 1$
6. about 5 	$6 + 7$ $8 - 2$ $10 - 1$
7. about 10	$6 + 3$ $12 - 6$ $9 - 2$
8. about 15 	$4 + 5$ $9 - 3$ $2 + 12$

© Harcourt

Ins and Outs

Write the missing numbers.
Then write the rule.

1.

In	Out
11	10
14	13
17	16
20	19
18	17

Subtract 1

2.

In	Out
10	
9	12
7	10
	11
6	9

_____

3.

In	Out
19	19
14	14
	18
16	16
17	

_____

4.

In	Out
18	9
	7
17	8
15	6
19	

_____

© Harcourt

Name _____

LESSON 20.2

Fill the Space

Write the missing numbers.
Use fact families to help.

1. $4 + \boxed{9} = 13$ $13 - \boxed{} = 9$ $\begin{array}{r} 13 \\ -\boxed{} \\ \hline 4 \end{array}$

2. $15 - \boxed{} = 9$ $15 - \boxed{} = 6$ $\begin{array}{r} 9 \\ +\boxed{} \\ \hline 15 \end{array}$

3. $7 + \boxed{} = 16$ $16 - \boxed{} = 7$ $\begin{array}{r} 16 \\ -\boxed{} \\ \hline 9 \end{array}$

4. $9 + \boxed{} = 19$ $19 - \boxed{} = 10$ $\begin{array}{r} 10 \\ +\boxed{} \\ \hline 19 \end{array}$

5. $\boxed{} + 8 = 17$ $\boxed{} - 8 = 9$ $\begin{array}{r} \boxed{} \\ + \ 9 \\ \hline 17 \end{array}$

6. $\boxed{} - 3 = 9$ $\boxed{} - 9 = 3$ $\begin{array}{r} \boxed{} \\ + \ 3 \\ \hline 12 \end{array}$

CW100   Challenge

© Harcourt

Arctic Art

Color [blue]▷ the spaces that show a way to make 16 or 17.
Color [yellow]▷ the spaces that show a way to make 18.
Don't color the spaces that show a way to make 19.
Color [black]▷ the spaces that show a way to make 20.

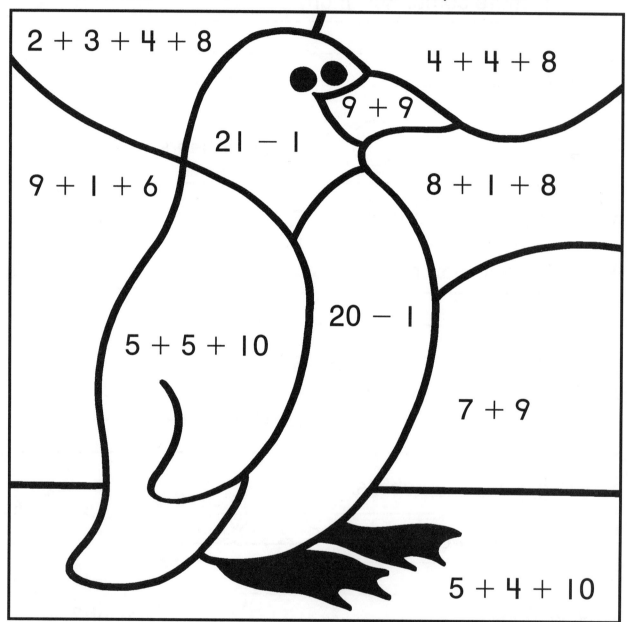

$2 + 3 + 4 + 8$

$4 + 4 + 8$

$9 + 9$

$21 - 1$

$9 + 1 + 6$

$8 + 1 + 8$

$5 + 5 + 10$

$20 - 1$

$7 + 9$

$5 + 4 + 10$

_____

What animal is this? _____

© Harcourt

Name _____

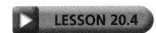

Write the Words

Complete the word problem. Then solve.

1. There are _____ polar bears.

   _____ more come. How many

   _____

   -

   polar _____ are there now?

   _____ ◯ _____ ◯ _____ polar bears

---

2. There are _____ snowmen.

   _____ melt. How many

   -

   _____ are left?

   _____ ◯ _____ ◯ _____ snowmen

---

3. There are _____ rabbits.

   _____ hop away.

   _____

   -

   How many _____ are left?

   _____ ◯ _____ ◯ _____ rabbits

© Harcourt

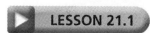

Spell It Out

How is your work?
Circle the pictures that show halves.
Circle their letters in the chart below.
Write the circled letters in order on the blanks.

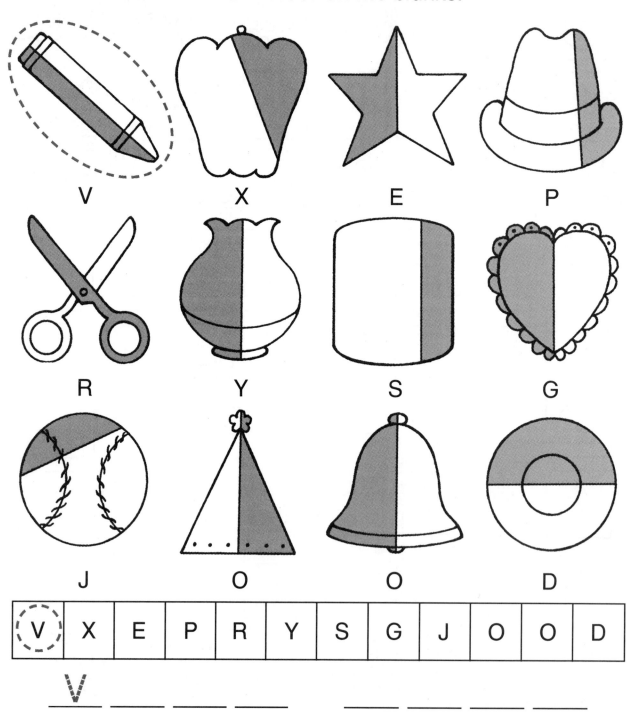

| V | X | E | P | R | Y | S | G | J | O | O | D |

V _ _ _ _ _ _ _   _ _ _ _

© Harcourt

Find the Way

Make a path from school to home.
Color the shapes that show fourths.

© Harcourt

Name _____

Making Fractions

Draw lines to show equal parts.
Then color the figure to show the fraction.

1.

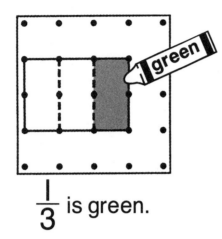

$\dfrac{1}{3}$ is green.

2.

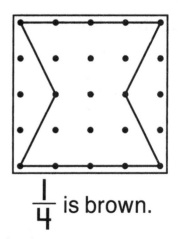

$\dfrac{1}{2}$ is blue.

3.

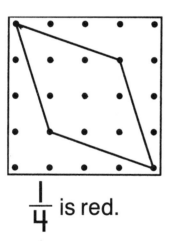

$\dfrac{1}{4}$ is red.

4.

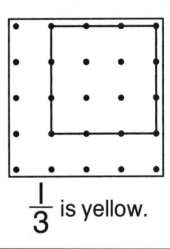

$\dfrac{1}{3}$ is yellow.

5.

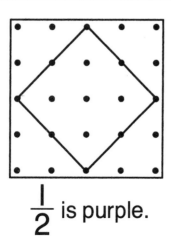

$\dfrac{1}{2}$ is purple.

6.

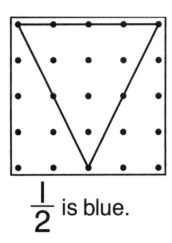

$\dfrac{1}{4}$ is brown.

© Harcourt

Look for Equal Parts

1. Look for 2 equal parts in the triangle.
   Trace lines with a crayon to show the parts.

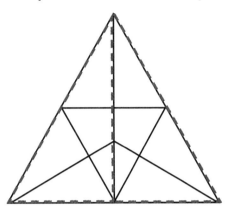

2. Look for 3 equal parts in the triangle.
   Trace lines with a crayon to show the parts.

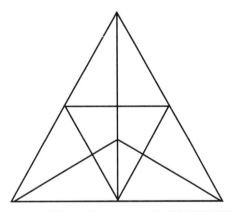

3. Look for 4 equal parts in the triangle.
   Trace lines with a crayon to show the parts.

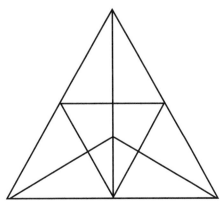

© Harcourt

What Fraction?

Use the picture. Circle the fraction.

1. Jeff eats 3 meals every day.
   Today he has eaten breakfast. He
   has not eaten lunch or dinner.
   What fraction of his meals has
   Jeff eaten?

   $\frac{1}{2}$ $\left(\frac{1}{3}\right)$ $\frac{1}{4}$

2. My dog has 4 legs.
   One of its legs is spotted.
   The other legs are black.
   What fraction of my dog's
   legs are spotted?

   $\frac{1}{2}$ $\frac{1}{3}$ $\frac{1}{4}$

3. Anna, Emily, and Molly are sisters.
   Emily is wearing a hat. Anna and
   Molly are not wearing hats.
   What fraction of the sisters
   are wearing hats?

   $\frac{1}{2}$ $\frac{1}{3}$ $\frac{1}{4}$

© Harcourt

Let's Go Shopping!

Draw pennies and nickels
to show how much each food costs.

1.

2.

3.

4.

© Harcourt

Name _____

Toy Town

Draw the number of dimes and
pennies you need to buy each toy.

1.  51¢

2.  22¢

3.  70¢

4. 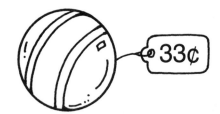 33¢

5.  81¢

© Harcourt

How Much Money?

Draw pennies, nickels, and dimes
to solve each problem.

1. Paco has 2 dimes. He finds 1 penny. How much money does Paco have now? __21__ ¢	
2. Lee has 3 dimes, 1 nickel, and 4 pennies. How much money does Lee have in all? _____ ¢	
3. Gwen has 1 dime and 1 nickel. Her mother gives her 1 nickel and 3 pennies. How much money does Gwen have now? _____ ¢	
4. Carlos has 7 pennies in his pocket. He has 7 nickels in his hand. How much money does Carlos have in all? _____ ¢	
5. Mike has 5 dimes. He saves 2 nickels and 2 pennies. How much money does Mike have now? _____ ¢	

© Harcourt

Name _____

Missing Coins

You need more coins to buy each thing.
Draw the coins you need.

1.

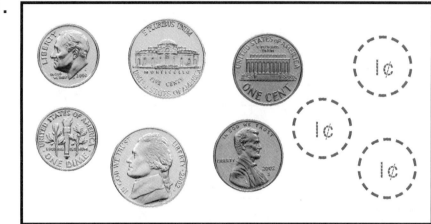 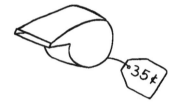

2.

 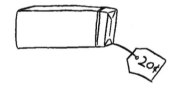

3.

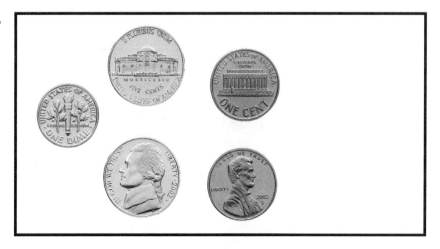 

© Harcourt

What Is It Worth?

List all the amounts you can make with the coins.

1.

5 ¢   10 ¢

15 ¢   20 ¢

2.

_____ ¢   _____ ¢

_____ ¢   _____ ¢

_____ ¢

3.

_____ ¢   _____ ¢

_____ ¢   _____ ¢

_____ ¢   _____ ¢   _____ ¢

© Harcourt

It's in the Bank!

You have these coins.	Use nickels and dimes. Trade for the fewest coins. Draw the coins.
1. 10	10¢
2. 35	
3. 20	
4. 30	
5. 45	

© Harcourt

Quarter Fun

1. Mack has one coin that equals 25¢.
Circle the coin.

2. Now he has 2 coins that equal 30¢.
Circle the coins.

3. Now he has 2 coins that equal 35¢.
Circle the coins.

4. Now he has 3 coins that equal 27¢.
Circle the coins.

5. Now he has 4 coins that equal 46¢.
Circle the coins.

© Harcourt

Riddle

"How is a person like this clock?"

Here is how to find out.

For 1–4, circle the picture if the coins equal a half dollar.
For 5–8, circle the picture if the coins equal a dollar.
Then write the letters in order at the bottom of the page.

1. 3 (quarter) 2 (dime)	**2.** 2 (quarter, circled)	**3.** 2 (quarter) 5 (penny)	**4.** 3 (dime) 4 (nickel)
T	**H**	**W**	**A**
5. 3 (quarter) 25 (penny)	**6.** 4 (quarter)	**7.** 2 (quarter) 3 (nickel)	**8.** 3 (quarter) 5 (nickel)
N	**D**	**E**	**S**

Answer: They both have __H__ ___ ___ ___ ___.

© Harcourt

Name _____

Money Maze

Trace the path.
Move to a square with a greater amount.

START

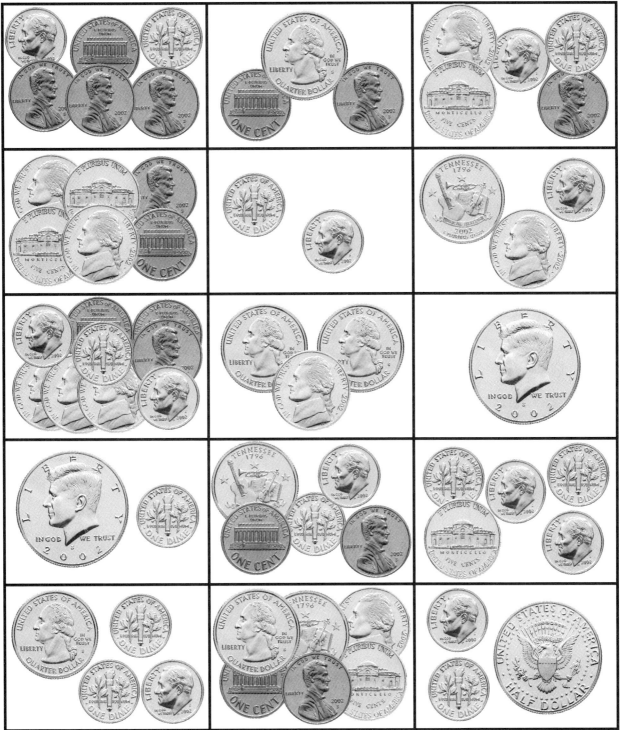

FINISH

© Harcourt

Name _____

Fewer Coins

Show the amount in two ways.
Circle the way that uses fewer coins.

1.

	dimes	nickels	pennies
15¢	(1	1)	
15¢		2	5

2.

	dimes	nickels	pennies
30¢			
30¢			

3.

	dimes	nickels	pennies
28¢			
28¢			

4.

	dimes	nickels	pennies
25¢			
25¢			

5.

	dimes	nickels	pennies
35¢			
35¢			

© Harcourt

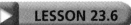

How Much More Do You Need?

Go shopping. Use coins to solve.

You have these coins.	You want to buy these things.	Draw the fewest coins to show how much more money you need.
1. (dime, penny, penny, penny)	(car) 15¢	(1¢) (1¢)
2. (dime, dime, dime, nickel)	(roller skate) 45¢	
3. (dime, dime, nickel, nickel, nickel)	(drum) 42¢	
4. (nickel, nickel, nickel, nickel, nickel)	(rocket) 36¢	

© Harcourt

Name _____

Tell Me When

My School Day			
9 o'clock	Reading	1 o'clock	Science
10 o'clock	Spelling	2 o'clock	Social Studies
11 o'clock	Math	3 o'clock	Go Home
12 o'clock	Lunch		

Circle the clock that shows the time for each activity.

1. Eat lunch.

2. Take a spelling test.

3. Open a math book.

4. Go home.

© Harcourt

Challenge **CW119**

Name _____

How Many Minutes?

Estimate how many minutes it will take.
Then act it out to see if you are correct.
Use a clock to time how long it takes.

1. Build a block tower.

Estimate

_____ minutes

My time

_____ minutes

2. Draw a picture of your family.

Estimate

_____ minutes

My time

_____ minutes

3. Do 10 sit-ups.

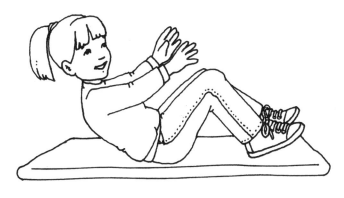

Estimate

_____ minutes

My time

_____ minutes

© Harcourt

Name _____

Hands on Time

Draw the hour and minute hands so that
both clocks show the same time.

1.

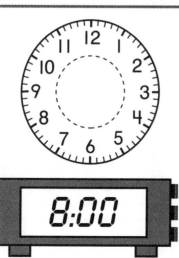

10:00

2.

6:00

3.

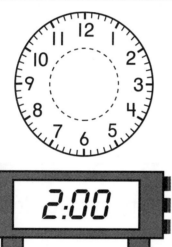

2:00

4.

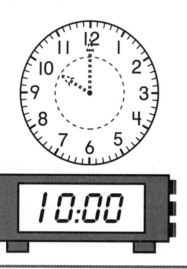

5:00

5.

8:00

6.

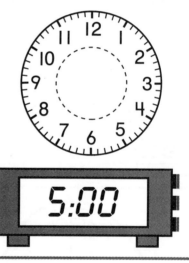

1:00

© Harcourt

Challenge **CW121**

Thirty Minutes Later

Look at the clock.
Write the time it will be thirty minutes later.

1.

Thirty minutes later

2.

Thirty minutes later

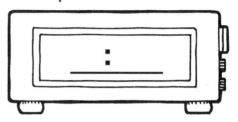

3.

Thirty minutes later

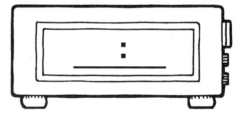

4.

Thirty minutes later

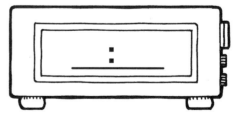

5.

Thirty minutes later

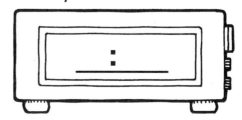

© Harcourt

Name _____

Time Trek

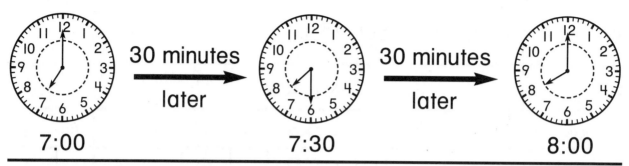

7:00 → 30 minutes later → 7:30 → 30 minutes later → 8:00

Draw a path from **Start** to **Finish**.
Each clock on the path shows 30 minutes later.

© Harcourt

Challenge **CW123**

Name _____

Date Book

Write the events on the calendar.

February						
Sunday	Monday	Tuesday	Wednesday	Thursday	Friday	Saturday
1	2	3	4	5	6	7
8	9	10	11	12	13	14
15	16	17	18	19	20	21
22	23	24	25	26	27	28

1. You go to the dentist on February 9.

2. There is a party on the first Saturday of the month.

3. You go to the zoo the day after the party.

4. You have piano lessons every Wednesday.

5. You have a day off on the last Monday of the month.

6. You are in a play on February 13 and one week later.

© Harcourt

What Comes Next?

Draw what might happen next.

1.

2.

3.

© Harcourt

Favorite Foods

15 children talked about their favorite foods.

Joel and Dena like chicken fingers.

Mike, Carrie, Shane, Brian, Kay, and Kim like pizza.

Chris, Maria, Kate, and Jamal like tacos.

Erin, Paco, and Hector like burgers.

1. Make a picture graph that shows the children's favorite foods.

Our Favorite Foods			
6			
5			
4			
3			
2			
1			
0			
chicken fingers	pizza	tacos	burgers

2. Write a question that someone can answer
   by reading this graph.

_____

_____

_____

© Harcourt

Tom's Day at School

Tom forgot to write the names of his subjects.
Use the clues to help you complete his chart.

1. Tom has Science first.

2. Reading lasts the longest amount of time.

3. Math ends at 10:30.

4. Art lasts one hour.

5. Lunch comes after Art and before Reading.

Subject	Start	End
Science	9:00	10:00
	10:00	10:30
	10:30	11:30
	11:30	12:00
	12:00	2:00

© Harcourt

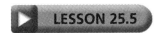

How Long?

Color the box **red** ⬅ if the activity takes about one minute.

Color the box **blue** ⬅ if it takes about one hour.

Clean your room.

Button a coat.

Play a game of soccer.

Drink milk.

Jump rope.

Cut out a shape.

Wash your hands.

Watch a play.

Sing the ABCs.

© Harcourt

Which Is Longer?

Circle the longer squiggle.
Use string to measure.

1.

 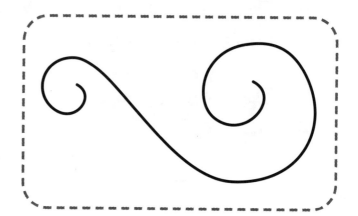

2.

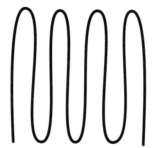 

3.

© Harcourt

Longer or Shorter

1. Meg's doll shoe is longer than Jill's.

   Estimate how many  long each shoe is.

   Use 📎 to measure. Color Meg's shoe ▐ **blue** ▐▷.

   Color Jill's shoe ▐ **red** ▐▷.

Estimate: about _____ 📎   Estimate: about _____ 📎

Measure: about _____ 📎   Measure: about _____ 📎

2. Sam's toy car is shorter than David's.

   Estimate how many 📎 long each car is.

   Use 📎 to measure. Color Sam's car ▐ **green** ▐▷.

   Color David's car ▐ **yellow** ▐▷.

Estimate: about _____ 📎   Estimate: about _____ 📎

Measure: about _____ 📎   Measure: about _____ 📎

© Harcourt

Measure Me

Use an inch ruler to measure. Then compare.

1. Measure your foot and your hand.

   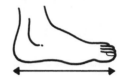

_____ inches   _____ inches

Which is longer? _____

---

2. Measure your pinky and your thumb.

_____ inches   _____ inches

Which is longer? _____

---

3. Measure your leg and your arm.

_____ inches   _____ inches

Which is longer? _____

---

4. Measure your big step and your jump.

_____ inches   _____ inches

Which is longer? _____

© Harcourt

Name _____

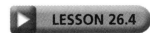

The Art Studio

Look around your classroom.
Draw 2 objects you measure in inches. Color them red.
Draw 2 objects you measure in feet. Color them blue.
Write a label for each object.

1. _____	2. _____
3. _____	4. _____

© Harcourt

Name _____

Go for the Stars

Use real objects and a centimeter ruler.
Estimate if each length is more or less than
10 centimeters. Color a star. Then measure.

Object	More Than 10 Centimeters	Less Than 10 Centimeters	Measure
1. ⬚	☆	☆	_____
2. ⬚	☆	☆	_____
3. ⬚	☆	☆	_____
4. ⬚	☆	☆	_____
5. ⬚	☆	☆	_____

© Harcourt

Challenge   CW133

Name _____

Estimate and Measure

Estimate. Draw if you need to.

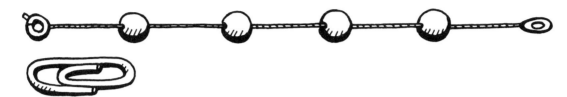

1. About how many 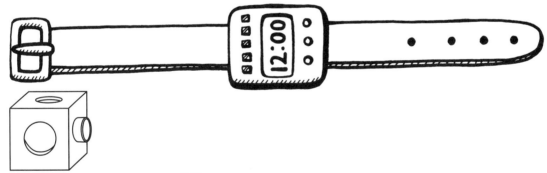 long is the bracelet?

   About __5__

2. About how many long are two bracelets?

   About _____

3. About how many long are three bracelets?

   About _____

4. About how many long is the watch?

   About _____

5. About how many long are two watches?

   About _____

6. About how many long are three watches?

   About _____

© Harcourt

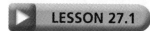

Apple Balance

Draw the correct number of apples to balance.

1.

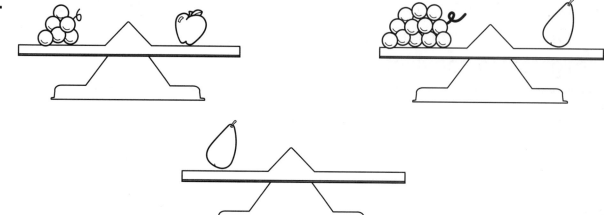

2.

3.

© Harcourt

Name _____

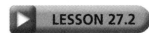

Weigh In

Find 4 items to weigh. Estimate how much each object weighs. Draw them in order from lightest to heaviest.	Use a balance to measure each object. Draw the objects in order again.

about _____ pounds	about _____ pounds
about _____ pounds	about _____ pounds
about _____ pounds	about _____ pounds
about _____ pounds	about _____ pounds

© Harcourt

Watermelon's Weighing In

The watermelon weighs about 2 kilograms.
Draw how many watermelons it will take
to balance each object.

1.

2.

3.

4.

© Harcourt

Name _____

Weigh to Go!

Predict the order of the objects from lightest to heaviest.
Number them from 1 to 4.
1 is the lightest. 4 is the heaviest.

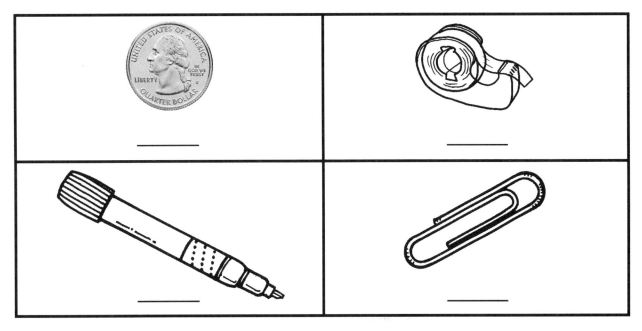

Measure each object.
Order and number the objects again.
Check your predictions.

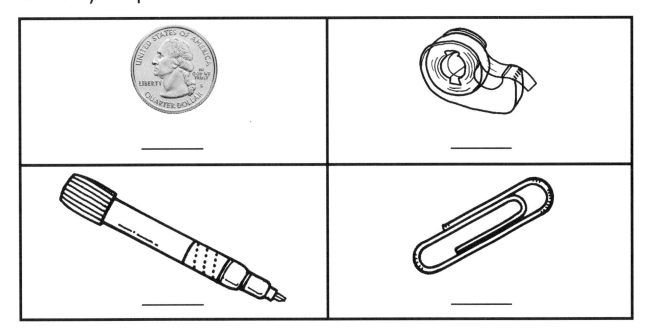

© Harcourt

Name _____

Go with the Flow

Circle the container that will fill first.
Draw an X on the container that will fill last.

1.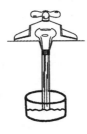

2.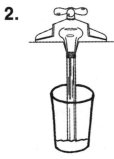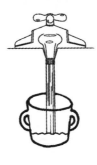

3.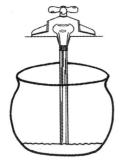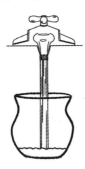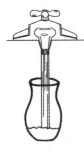

4.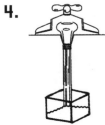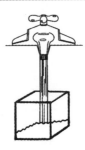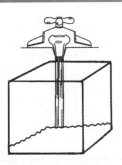

© Harcourt

How Many Cups?

Draw the number of cups that fill
the container or containers.
Write the number.

cup   pint   quart

1.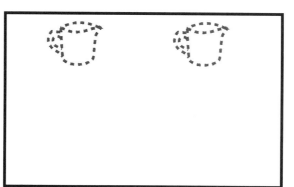

_4_ cups

2.

_____ cups

3.

_____ cups

© Harcourt

Color the Containers

Color **yellow** containers that hold less than 1 liter.
Color **orange** containers that hold about 1 liter.
Color **green** containers that hold more than 1 liter.

1.

2.

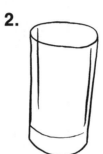

3.

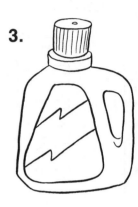

4.

5.

6.

7.

8.

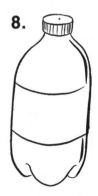

© Harcourt

Hotter and Colder

Color the thermometer to show the temperature.
What would you wear outside?
Draw a picture to show.

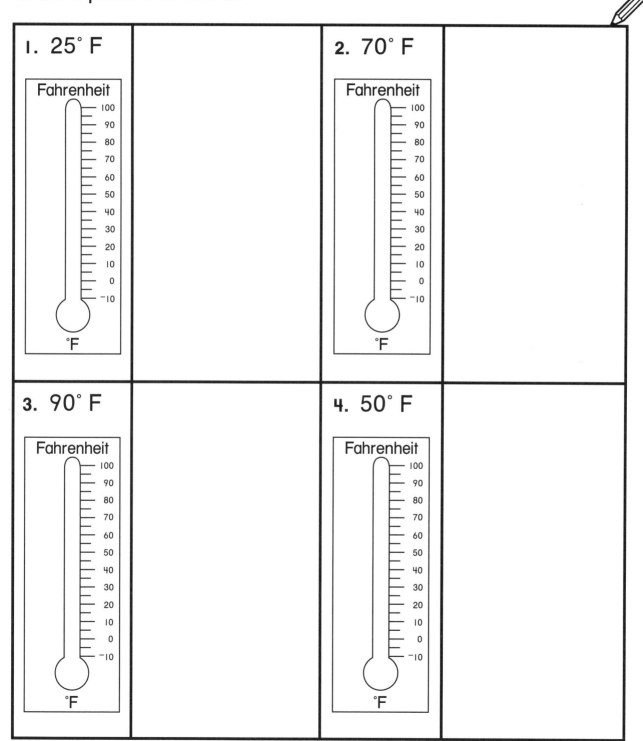

1. 25° F

Fahrenheit

°F

2. 70° F

Fahrenheit

°F

3. 90° F

Fahrenheit

°F

4. 50° F

Fahrenheit

°F

© Harcourt

Not the Same

Use ☕ , ▬▬▬ , and ⚖ to help you find the objects.
Draw the objects in the boxes.

1. Find two different objects that hold about the same amount. They should be different heights.

☐ and ☐

Circle the one that is higher.

2. Find two different objects that are about the same weight. They should be different lengths.

☐ and ☐

Circle the one that is longer.

3. Find two containers that are about the same height. They should hold different amounts.

☐ and ☐

Circle the one that holds more.

4. Find two objects that are about the same height. They should be different widths.

 and ☐

Circle the one that is wider.

© Harcourt

Find the Tens

Draw the missing ⬚⬚⬚⬚⬚. Write the missing numbers.

1.

___4___ tens + ___4___ tens = ___8___ tens = ___80___

2.

_____ tens + _____ tens = _____ tens = _____

3.

_____ tens + _____ tens = _____ tens = _____

4.

_____ tens + _____ tens = _____ tens = _____

CW144   Challenge

© Harcourt

Name _____

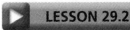

Find the Missing Numbers

Write the missing numbers.

1. $4 + \boxed{44} = 48$

2. $52 + \boxed{} = 58$

3. $23 + \boxed{} = 28$

4. $31 + \boxed{} = 34$

5. $\boxed{} + 4 = 37$

6. $\boxed{} + 6 = 29$

7. $\boxed{} + 5 = 56$

8. $46 + \boxed{} = 48$

9. $\boxed{} + 2 = 28$

10. $\boxed{} + 4 = 67$

11. $31 + \boxed{} = 35$

12. $\boxed{} + 3 = 55$

13. $28 + \boxed{} = 29$

14. $\boxed{} + 4 = 68$

15. $\boxed{} + 1 = 47$

16. $56 + 2 = \boxed{}$

17. $34 + \boxed{} = 39$

18. $35 + \boxed{} = 38$

© Harcourt

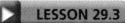

Missing Prices

Write the missing price.

1. 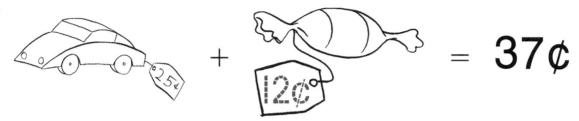 = **37¢**

2.   = **45¢**

3. 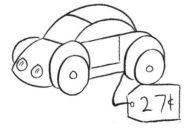  = **59¢**

4.   = **49¢**

5. = **62¢**

© Harcourt

Name _____

Subtract and Spell

Who lives in the house?

- Subtract tens. Write the missing numbers.
- Use the code box. Write the letter on the blank below the problem.
- Read the word you spell.
- Draw the animal in the house.

Code Box						
10	20	30	40	50	60	70
o	e	s	u	m	t	a

1. $\begin{array}{r} 60 \\ -\ 10 \\ \hline \boxed{50} \end{array}$

2. $\begin{array}{r} 80 \\ -\ 70 \\ \hline \boxed{} \end{array}$

3. $\begin{array}{r} 70 \\ -\ \boxed{} \\ \hline 30 \end{array}$

4. $\begin{array}{r} 90 \\ -\ \boxed{} \\ \hline 60 \end{array}$

5. $\begin{array}{r} 40 \\ -\ 20 \\ \hline \boxed{} \end{array}$

m   ___   ___   ___   ___

A _____ lives in the house!

© Harcourt

Name _____

Subtraction Scramble

Write − and = to complete the subtraction problems.
Color the boxes. Look across and down.
Not all numbers will be used.

36	−	4	=	32	25		87		7		80
		21				22		19			23
12	29			66		44				44	
−	2	10		5			55			3	10
	27			61			3			41	
56		22	15				52		29		48
	10		1		9				6		
42							37		23		16
99		1		98			2			18	
		34		17		35		12		74	
	23							82			2
	2	57		3		54					72
	21		59						25		
73			15			39		3		36	

CW148   Challenge

© Harcourt

Make Change

Pay with the coins.
Write the amount of change.

1.

 — (apple) 30¢ = ___20___ ¢

2.

 — (quilt) 21¢ = _____ ¢

3.

 — (jacks) 36¢ = _____ ¢

4.

 — (bear) 50¢ = _____ ¢

© Harcourt

Rainforest Bird

Estimate.

Use the key to color the toucan.

Key

about 10 = black	about 30 = green	about 50 = rainbow
about 80 = red	about 100 = yellow	

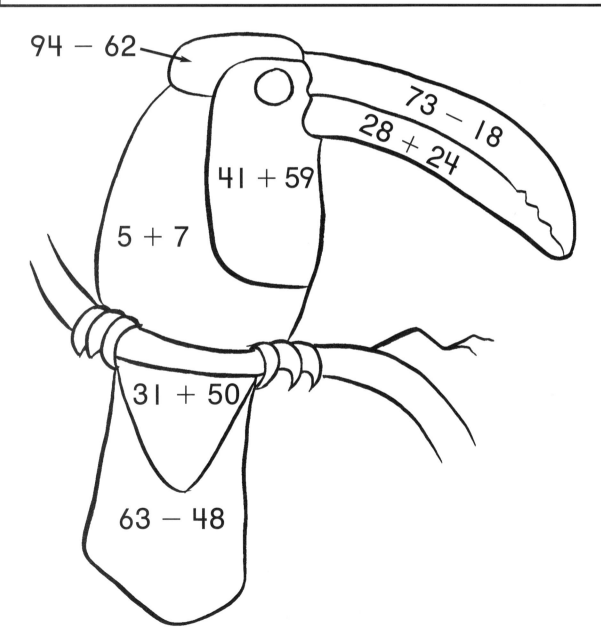

$94 - 62$

$73 - 18$

$28 + 24$

$41 + 59$

$5 + 7$

$31 + 50$

$63 - 48$

© Harcourt

Name _____

For All the Marbles

Color the marbles in each bag to
make the sentence true.

1. It is impossible to pull
   a green marble from
   the bag.

2. It is certain to pull
   a red marble from the
   bag.

3. It is impossible to pull
   a blue marble from
   the bag.

4. It is certain to pull a yellow
   marble from the bag.

5. It is certain to pull
   a green marble from
   the bag.

6. It is impossible to pull a
   blue marble from the bag.

© Harcourt

Name _____

Odd or Even?

Which kind of number is more likely on the next spin?
Circle **odd** or **even**.

1.

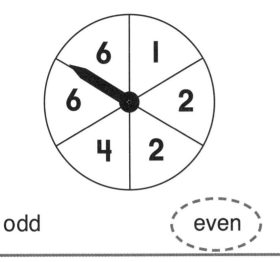

odd   (even)

2.

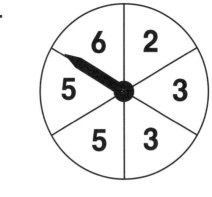

odd   even

3.

odd   even

4.

odd   even

5.

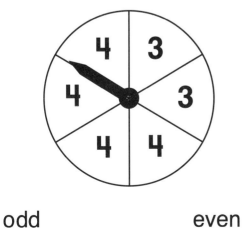

odd   even

6.

odd   even

© Harcourt

Name _____

Equally Likely Shapes

Draw ☐ so that ☐ and
△ are equally likely.

1.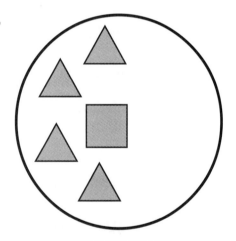

2.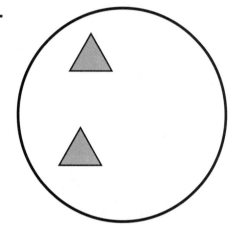

3.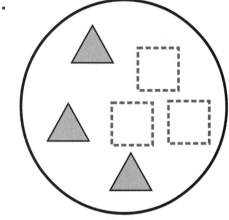

4.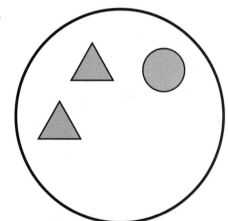

5.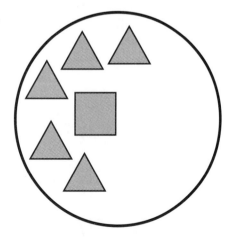

6.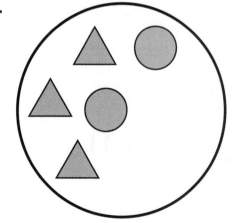

© Harcourt

Predict More or Less

Write **more** or **less**.

1.

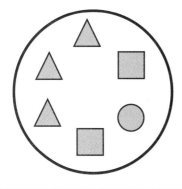

△ is _____ likely than ▢

▢ is _____ likely than ◯

▢ is _____ likely than △

2.

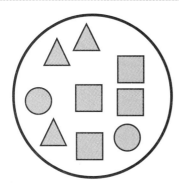

◯ is _____ likely than ▢

△ is _____ likely than ▢

▢ is _____ likely than △

3.

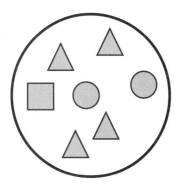

▢ is _____ likely than ◯

△ is _____ likely than ◯

◯ is _____ likely than △

4.

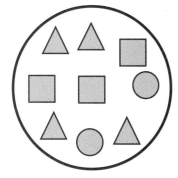

▢ is _____ likely than ◯

◯ is _____ likely than ▢

◯ is _____ likely than △

© Harcourt